Child-centred Education

Child-centred Education

HAROLD ENTWISTLE

METHUEN & CO LTD
11 New Fetter Lane · London EC4

First published 1970
by Methuen & Co. Ltd
© *1970 Harold Entwistle*
Printed in Great Britain
by Ebenezer Baylis & Son Ltd
The Trinity Press
Worcester and London

SBN 416 13760 1

Distributed in the U.S.A.
by Barnes & Noble Inc.

for Giles

Contents

7

Acknowledgements

This text is an adaptation of materials forming part of a Ph.D. thesis, *The Concept of Activity in Education*, accepted by the University of London in 1966. In rewriting this material for a more general readership I have had the benefit of valuable critical comments from the following friends and colleagues who have read all or parts of the manuscript: Jeanette Coltham, Ken Dagnall, David Hargreaves, Eric Hoyle, Philip Jackson, John Naylor, Geof Roberts, Raymond Ryba, Phil Walking and Keith Whalley. My grateful thanks are due to these and to my wife, who has also assisted with the numerous secretarial chores inseparable from work of this kind.

1 : Introduction:
Child-centred education

It is sometimes argued that the child-centred emphasis in education is at least as old as Plato's prescription, 'Let your children's education take the form of play'. But whilst most educational systems have recognized that some concession must be made to children's intellectual limitations, it was with Rousseau that there entered into educational thought a completely new emphasis which Dewey likened to a Copernican revolution: 'the old education . . . may be summed up by stating that the center of gravity is outside the child. It is in the teacher, the textbook, anywhere and everywhere you please except in the immediate instincts and activities of the child himself . . . Now the change which is coming into education is the shifting of the center of gravity . . . the child becomes the sun about which they are organized.'[1] This emphasis upon the child has been a recurrent theme in educational literature over the past two centuries. 'Child-centred education' has thus become a slogan with all the potential for promoting change and creating misunderstanding which is characteristic of sloganmongering in education, as in politics or the arts.[2] Not surprisingly, it has provoked a critical, even hostile, reception from many educationists. However, what is attempted in this text is neither an apologia for child-centred education nor an attack upon this tradition but, rather, an attempt to escape from some of the unreal either–or dilemmas into which both child-centred theorists and their critics often want to force us. The intention is to sift the arguments and clarify the issues which arise when we bring the learner into the centre of our attention and to examine some of the conceptual distinctions which have to be made if the idea of child-centred education is to be a useful instrument in the theory and practice of education.

The impression that we are confronted with exclusive choices in education (for example, 'children not subjects', child versus teacher, subjects or the integrated curriculum, individual or society, freedom versus discipline, etc.) has perhaps been fostered by the strong resistance the child-centred movement has encountered. This has arisen partly from the stubborn refusal of a majority of teachers to embrace child-centred doctrines and practices, and partly from the sort of backlash exemplified by the recent Black Paper, *Fight for Education*.[3] Some critics tend to see in child-centred education the source of all society's ills: everything from illiteracy to violent crime is debited against the progressive educationist's pre-occupation with the values of childhood as against those of the mature and responsible adult members of the community. The authors of the Black Paper wrote as though they had discovered a new and malignant growth within the body educational, and the illusion that the document was saying something novel was underlined by Mr Edward Short (Secretary of State, Department of Education and Science) who pronounced the document's publication 'the blackest day in English education for over a century'. In fact, the Black Paper epitomizes nothing more than the perennial conviction of the ageing that nothing in the universe is quite what it used to be. As such it is nothing new. A decade before the appearance of the Black Paper, Jacques Barzun denounced 'education without instruction' which issues in 'no knowledge that is precise and firm, no ability to do intellectual work with thoroughness and despatch'. He catalogued the consequent deficiences of college graduates who 'cannot read accurately or write clearly, cannot do percentages or fractions without travail and doubt, cannot utter their thoughts with fluency or force, can rarely show a handwriting that would pass for adult, let alone legible, cannot trust themselves to use the foreign language they have studied for eight years . . .' and so on.[4] Although this criticism referred to American education, Barzun saw European education going the same way. But forty years ago Godfrey Thompson wrote: 'In commercial circles a common criticism of the schools has been, for certainly twenty years and perhaps more, that they no longer attend to the three Rs thoroughly as in the good old days, but fritter their time away with all sorts of fancy subjects'.[5] This puts the backlash in Britain as far back as the turn of the century. And although Barzun implies that before 1900 the child-centred malaise had not afflicted American schools,[6] Butts and Cremin note the existence of mid-nineteenth-century diatribes against the corrupting influence of the 'new' education: 'In general, three reasons were cited for the utter failure of public education: *first*, a curriculum full of frills like art and music which detracted from teaching of the essentials; *second*, the absolute decadence of the teaching of English; and *third*, the tendency of modern education to make study too easy, too entertaining'. The remedy advanced was simple: 'a return to a curriculum which demanded of the students practice and skill in the essential subjects of language and arithmetic'.[7]

That this invective against child-centred education has to be renewed afresh with almost every generation suggests that there is something valuable and enduring in the tradition, an assumption underlined by the fact that child-centred education is not merely the plaything of a lunatic fringe; it has become institutionalized and is official policy in many educational systems. In 1921, for example, the Superintendent of Schools in Berlin declared that 'All youth have a right to a happy life in school'.[8] In Britain this article of faith was the basis of the 1944 Education Act[9] as it was also of more recent Scandinavian school reforms.[10] And this notion that children should be happy in school has brought real educational gains. School discipline is rarely the repressive, even brutal, thing it often was a century ago. Teachers are much more approachable than they once were and children are no longer expected to be seen but not heard. Undoubtedly schools are happier places for being child-centred. Despite the sombre pictures of some contemporary secondary schools painted by Hargreaves[11] and Partridge,[12] and however much some child-centred educationists believe that schools have remained largely unaffected by their crusade, there is a world of difference between today's schools and those of a century ago portrayed fictionally by Dickens or in the reports of Matthew Arnold, H.M.I.[13]

Nevertheless, the fact that the tradition of protest against the alleged evils of child-centredness is as persistent as the movement itself suggests that the 'backlash' is rooted in genuine concern at what seem to be the excesses and omissions of those who locate the child at the centre of the educational situation. A particular danger seems to lie in the literal and slavish application of child-centred slogans. Contemporary critics have not been slow to seize on these, often ignoring the contexts which gave the slogans their initial relevance. Others, not unsympathetic to the aims of child-centred educationists, have warned of the dangers of an exclusive emphasis upon the child. There exists the danger of not taking sufficient thought about the curriculum (see Chapter 6). Or there is sometimes too limited a conception of what the child is capable of learning: whilst emphasizing the child's right to happiness and freedom from the contraints of adult life, we are under an obligation to form an adequate conception of what he is capable of learning at a given stage of development (see Chapter 5). Again, perhaps child-centred educationists are in danger of sentimentalizing childhood. How far does the stress upon the child come from wanting to prolong his innocence – to delay his growing up, not for his own sake but for ours? Is there an element of adult self-indulgence in all this?

Whilst not wishing to create unhappiness in schools where children spend the major portion of their waking lives, some critics argue that the obsession with children's happiness elevates to the status of an educational aim something which can only be an accompanying condition of schooling.[14] Others wonder if there really ever can be education without tears. In their view the *mastery* of human knowledge and skill requires disciplined application to repetitive drills and procedures which (whatever the glow of satisfaction they ultimately induce) must seem tedious in the event and far enough removed from the conventional view of what constitutes a happy state of affairs. Those critics who believe that the educational reaction in favour of the child has diminished the care for disciplined learning fear for standards of scholarship and even for literacy itself. The failure of some children to learn to read or write or calculate (and the belief that the average man does not possess these skills as competently as he once did) is debited against child-centred methods. Encouraged to do as they please (the popular epitome of child-centred classrooms), few choose to make the effort to master the symbolic processes and most are content with second best. Against this view, and so far as there is any validity in the common belief that our educational achievements are not good enough, child-centred educationists might well retort that the continuing impoverished standards of mass education stem from our failure to apply, with sufficient insight or enthusiasm, those discoveries about the child and his nature which have been the product of developmental psychology. It is not that child-centred education has been tried and found wanting; it has never really been tried. In particular, defenders of this tradition would argue that in pursuit of literacy and numeracy, schools have mistakenly over-emphasized symbolic and abstract operations to the neglect of those concrete experiences which are necessarily antecedent to the mastery of abstractions: in Piagetian terms, formal-operational learning has taken over prematurely from concrete experience. The authors of the Black Paper have emphasized the importance of getting behind the sentimental platitudes about education to the facts of what is really happening in schools. But in fact, evidence on this question of how far schools have become child-centred is almost impossible to come by. A child-centred or progressive school is a quite subjective notion and it is difficult to envisage how any criteria of child-centredness which might be agreed could be susceptible to statistical measurement. It is ironic that though the authors of the Black Paper set much store by the facts, there is hardly a fact in the entire document. One's impression is that our primary schools have not been taken over by the progressives to anything like the extent these conservatives would have us believe. Far from being hotbeds of progressivism, 'chalk and talk' still accurately describes teaching methods in the majority of schools and child-centred educationists might cogently argue, from the facts, that if our educational standards are as appallingly inadequate as the critics maintain, it is educational conservatism rather than progressive education which is at the root of the problem.

Other critics of child-centred education argue that the emphasis upon happiness in schools ignores the essentially tragic character of human life (see pages 83–4). Too much freedom in education is believed to dispose the child towards an unhealthy egocentric view of experience. Children are unwilling to accept reasonable authority. The untutored values, preferences and whims of children are elevated above the mature, experienced judgements of parents, priests, teachers and others who might expect to evoke respect from the young. The related problems of freedom, authority and discipline are clearly central to an evaluation of child-centred education (see Chapter 4).

It is also important to ask how far the child's *present* interests and needs should determine his curriculum (see Chapter 5). Is there anything to commend Rousseau's conviction that education which is concerned with preparation for future life is a waste of time for both teacher and child? How far are the child's interests served by encouraging a preoccupation with his personal interests and problems; with life as *he* sees it? In what sense, if any, can preparation for the future be reconciled with the requirement that schooling should have meaning for the child as and when it happens? Does the idea of the autonomy of the child's interests give an adequate account of what his present life might be or of what he is capable of becoming? How far do we need a concept of the educated man as well as (indeed, as a necessary correlate of) the notion of the educated child?

The relationship which should exist between the child and his teacher is fundamental to many of these questions (see Chapter 9). Some child-centred educationists adopt the extreme view that any manifestation of teaching is a threat to the child's integrity as a person. A somewhat less radical conclusion is that ultimately no one can teach anyone else anything: that whatever the teacher's role in the educational process, the child is ultimately the agent of his own education. This concept of the self-activated learner merits sympathetic examination before one

concludes with Barzun that we are 'witnessing an abdication of
the teaching power . . . if all teaching is self teaching, then the
schools are wasting even more of the country's money than I
suspect'.[15] For to stress the importance in learning of self
activity may be to underline the essential individuality of the
learner as a mind with its own peculiar history, characterized by
a unique complex of gifts and limitations. That we should meet
the child as an individual is a cardinal principle of child-centred
education. This individualistic emphasis often seems at odds
with our current preoccupation with social objectives in education. In what sense is the cultivation of individuality an acceptable educational aim and how valid is the perennial fear that
society constitutes a threat to individual integrity? (see Chapters
2 and 3.)

In attempting to disentangle these strands which are woven
into the concept of child-centred education, it will be useful to
mark a different kind of distinction which cuts across most of
these issues. It is necessary to distinguish between normative
and technical educational prescriptions. On the one hand, child-
centred educationists inherit a collection of moral aphorisms
about childhood: on the other, there are propositions about
learning and child development whose justification depends
upon empirical evidence. Much of the emphasis upon the child
has been prompted by psychological insights into the learning
processes and the way in which concepts develop in the maturing
individual. Here the problems are empirical or technical: what
is it possible to teach children at different ages and how do we
best undertake the task of teaching them those things which they
are capable of learning? In recent years, particularly following
dissemination of the work of Piaget and his followers, the
interest in the child has been mainly technical in this sense. But
the initial concentration of attention upon the child was a moral
protest against the abuse of childhood; an outcry against treating the child as a means to an end – even the end of his own
future happiness or well being. That is, it was a protest in the
tradition of Rousseau against education conceived merely as a
preparation for the future and a preoccupation with what it
means to be an educated man at the expense of due consideration

2

of the child's interests and aspirations as a child. Despite Rousseau's interest in stages of development which foreshadows the Piagetian developmental psychology, and Pestalozzi's and Froebel's search for method, each began with affirmations about the nature of childhood and denunciations of traditional child-rearing methods which were couched in the language of morals. Thus, the child-centred movement in education can be viewed as an aspect of the wider movement to extend the notion of human rights to categories of human beings who had hitherto been denied respect as persons: factory hands, women, slaves and subject peoples. In one way or another, each of these groups was regarded as existing only instrumentally to serve the purposes of others. The movements for factory reform, abolition of slavery and emancipation of women derived their impetus from the moral imperative to afford human rights to these various underprivileged categories of person. On similar grounds, child-centred educationists have stressed that children have a right to consideration and treatment as intrinsically valuable human beings. In educational theory it is important to try to separate the moral from the technical prescriptions since these require quite different modes of evaluation: this distinction is drawn in a number of contexts in our discussion.

As we have noted, some of the educational emphases which are encapsulated in this persuasion to focus upon the child have been subject to sustained attack by critics of this tradition. Nevertheless, it is impossible to teach in any educational institution, at whatever level, as though these ideas had never gained currency. In this connexion it is worth noting that all but one of our distinctions within the concept of child-centred education – the notion that the child ought to be considered *as a child* (see Chapter 5) – might apply to education at any stage. This could be taken as implying that the notion of *the educated child* reveals the essential meaning of child-centred education. However, other implications of this tradition – emphasis upon the individual learner and the problems this raises for social education, the insistence upon freedom, the sense in which learning might be said to be self-activated, the question of who defines the curriculum and its relationship with the life of the learner, the problem of justifying the teacher's authority and the very activity of teaching itself – these all involve considerations pertinent to the question of how far education at any age should be *learner-centred*. Some critics of child-centred education give the impression that they would be perfectly happy provided this approach were confined safely to the periphery of the educational system and applied only to the schooling of the very young or the very dull. However, though this discussion will be exemplified mainly by reference to schools, it has not been located within the sphere of primary education. For many of the frictions in secondary education and the disenchantment increasingly voiced by students in higher education stem from a failure to look at education from the learner's point of view. Hence, it is suggested that to sustain the interest of the reluctant adolescent we need to link schooling with life 'as he sees it'. Again, the dissatisfaction with lectures and the demands which are made for extended use of other methods of teaching in higher education (tutorials, seminars, practical activities) reflect earlier condemnation of 'talk and chalk' in schools and of the failure to enlist children's active participation in their education. Current student demands to be consulted about the content of their courses also raise the problem of authority in education. Campaigns for the institution of student control of examinations reflect long-standing criticisms of examination procedures in schools, especially by child-centred educationists. Indeed, problems of higher education are increasingly discussed in terms reminiscent of the vocabulary of the child-centred tradition. For example, the Hale Committee[16] noted student criticism of the lecture as an authoritarian 'one way' process (essentially the criticism of chalk and talk) and defined the distinction between tutorials and seminars as that between a student-centred and a subject-centred methodology. Asa Briggs's account of the experiments at Sussex leans on the concepts of activity, practical and instrumental education; and the cross-disciplinary character of the contextual studies he describes, together with his notion of education in the university as a 'personal quest', recalls advocacy of the integrated curriculum and the pedagogical efficacy of problem solving.[17] The insistence of students in colleges and departments of education that their courses should be designed to reflect practice as they find it in the schools has all the validity and the dangers of claims made for the efficacy of learning by doing (see pp. 151–3). Thus, many of the discontents which afflict upper secondary and higher education and the remedies currently prescribed for these ills have long been focused by critics of traditional educational procedures in the schools. Indeed, it is this sort of parallel between the panaceas prescribed for the problems of the primary schools and of the universities which agitates the authors of the Black Paper. Their complaint is that students do not merely bring to higher education the undisciplined minds which are a product of permissive practices in the primary school, but also expect the university to be conducted as though it were a primary school with the result that many university teachers are abdicating to the philosophy of student-centred education. Hence, although differences between stages of education cannot be ignored, most of the issues raised here must be the concern of teachers, whether their work is in the infant school or the university.

REFERENCES

1   J. DEWEY *School and Society*, p. 34. Phoenix Books, University of Chicago Press, 1959.
2   See I. SCHEFFLER *The Language of Education*, Ch. 2. C. C. Thomas, Springfield, Illinois, 1960.
3   C. B. COX and A. E. DYSON (Eds.) *Fight for Education, A Black Paper*. The Critical Quarterly Society, 1969.
4   J. BARZUN *The House of Intellect*, Ch. IV. Secker & Warburg, London, 1959.
5   G. H. THOMSON *A Modern Philosophy of Education*, p. 40. Allen & Unwin, London, 1929.
6   Ibid., p. 90.
7   R. F. BUTTS and L. A. CREMIN *A History of Education in American Culture*, pp. 386–7. Henry Holt, New York, 1953.
8   A. FERRIERE *The Activity School*, p. viii. Allen & Unwin, London, 1929.

9   BOARD OF EDUCATION *Educational Reconstruction.* White Paper Cmd. 6458, 1943.

10   See S. MARKLUND and P. SÖDERBERG *The Swedish Comprehensive School.* Longmans, London, 1967.

11   D. H. HARGREAVES *Social Relations in a Secondary School.* Routledge & Kegan Paul, London, 1967.

12   J. PARTRIDGE *Life in a Secondary Modern School.* Penguin Books, 1968.

13   M. ARNOLD *Reports on Elementary Schools* 1852–1882. H.M.S.O., London, 1910.

14   For a critical examination of the concept of 'Happiness in Education' see R. F. DEARDEN in *The Proceedings of the Philosophy of Education Society of Great Britain,* 1968.

15   BARZUN, op. cit., pp. 124–5.

16   UNIVERSITY GRANTS COMMITTEE *University Teaching Methods.* H.M.S.O., London, 1964.

17   A. BRIGGS 'Drawing a New Map of Learning' in D. DAICHES (Ed.) *The Idea of a New University.* André Deutsch, London, 1964.

2: The individual child

The child-centred movement in education grew as a protest 'against the old rigidly systematized school which imposed its procedure on all the pupils'.[1] It was founded on the assumption that 'the educational system exists first, last and always to serve the development of the child as an individual'.[2] However, the pedagogical implications of this stress upon individual development are not always as clearly drawn as they might be. R. S. Peters takes the view that this emphasis on individuality usually amounts to a warning against treating the child 'as merely a citizen in the making'.[3] But the plea that we should consider the *individual* child involves more than a recognition that the child is not an adult 'writ small' (see Chapter 5); more, that is, than the conviction that childhood itself is intrinsically valuable and, on that account, makes its own demands upon the educational system. No doubt children of the same age are likely to have common characteristics and needs which differentiate them from other age groups and these age differences should be taken into account if schooling is to be effective. The eight-year-old, as an eight-year-old, may have many things in common with all children of that age which are peculiar to eight-year-olds and to no other age group. But to stress the *individual* child is to believe that each child is unique in the complex of ability, aptitude, interest, experience and cultural capital which he brings into school. The teacher confronts every child as an individual having a unique personal history, by virtue of which his perception of the environment will be idiosyncratic. The skills, knowledge and disciplines which the school exists to disseminate must be assimilated within mental structures each of which is unique. To that extent the meaning of any fact, concept or principle will be distinctive and personal. As Sir Percy Nunn, a notable advocate of individualism as an educational ideal put it: 'While every man tends to draw his ideal of life largely from the inspiration of others, yet it may be maintained that, in a perfectly good sense of the words, each must have his own unique ideal'. It follows that 'there can be no universal aim of education if that aim is to include the assertion of any particular ideal of life; for there are as many ideals as there are persons'.[4]

This belief in the unique educational requirement of every individual has sometimes found practical expression in a curriculum based upon individual assignments: in principle, a different curriculum seems appropriate for every child. The best known example of this individualization of the curriculum is the Dalton Plan.[5] But schools whole-heartedly committed to this interpretation of educational individualism have been rare. A much commoner practice in schools has been to apply individual tuition to special categories of children (usually the backward or the handicapped) or to limited areas of the curriculum. In the first instance, the focus is upon the individual child's shortcomings and on the provision of remedial teaching designed to bring his achievement in the fundamental skills more nearly into line with that of the average or normal child. Otherwise, the linking of learning to individual differences has taken place in those subjects which are more obviously concerned with skill.

In physical education, for example, there is now a well-established practice of letting children find their own spaces in which to work instead of positioning them in ranks. This alteration of the formal arrangement of a class in physical education follows from the recognition that the rhythm which accompanies the efficient performance of most physical skills must be personal, related to the rhythm of an individual's vital processes. In straight lines, differences of timing are aesthetically unacceptable. But remaining 'in step' has no meaning when the ranks are broken: haphazard arrangements of children free the individual from the discipline of the group whilst retaining the notion of a group activity. Similarly in mathematics, individual work has grown in importance. Dienes concluded that in mathematics 'it is not likely that more than three children will work at the same pace and in roughly the same way'.[6] This trend in mathematics teaching has been facilitated by the development and widespread use of mathematical equipment designed to be used by individuals.

Along with these specific attempts to relate the pace and methods of learning to individual differences, there have been more general methodological approaches to the problem. The programming of a school curriculum on to job cards as described by A. W. Rowe[7] is a recent example of this. A similar merit is often claimed for teaching machines. An important part of the rationale of programmed learning is that it enables learners to work at their own pace and facilitates the direction of individual learners to a particular sequence in the programme either for remedial purposes or to accelerate the 'express' learner (see Chapter 9).

Focusing attention upon the individual learner may derive from either technical or moral considerations (for an outline of this technical–moral distinction see pp. 17–18 above). A teacher who stresses individuality may be attempting to follow the moral imperative to treat his pupils as ends and not, technically, as things. But it is also possible to be interested in individual differences merely in a technical sense, as a means towards the efficient learning and teaching of a *given* curriculum which may make no concessions to individual interests or talents. Again, the categorization of individuals in terms of their I.Q. is a morally neutral device. It could be used – and this was its initial *raison d'être* in English education – as an instrument of the moral prescription that we ought to provide maximum opportunity for individuals irrespective of their social origin. But, unfortunately, this measuring instrument is constantly in danger of exploitation as a technical device to sort sheep from goats in the interests of making the best possible use of the nation's available talent. The widespread aversion to intelligence testing is a reaction against the practice of identifying the individual's intellectual capacities, largely in order to service a system of selective schooling which *types* the child. In place of the individual child we get the scholarship child, the secondary modern child and, latterly, the Newsom child.

Those having a merely technical interest in the pedagogical problems posed by individual differences need not begin with any sort of value-judgement about the moral basis of individual education. It would be possible to employ individual approaches to children as a means towards more efficient teaching, without having any commitment to the view that individuals matter and ought to be valued in and for themselves. For example, a mathematics teacher could vary his approach to different children on the basis of his understanding of their peculiar difficulties with mathematical processes, whilst in pursuit of an aim which could be considered to be anti-individualistic; namely, from a concern to produce educated manpower required by the national economy. Or he might just be interested in the technical problems of teaching mathematics and have no strongly developed educational ethic. In either case he would be seeing his pupils as means, not ends. An obvious example of resort to individual tuition for primarily technical reasons is when industry or the armed forces use teaching machines as the instruments of 'crash programmes' designed to promote efficiency or economy in the organization in the shortest possible time. And a teacher who responds to the technical challenge posed by individual differences might adopt individual tuition whilst regretting the existence of the problem; life might be much easier if differences in ability did not exist, but since they do, efficient education demands that his teaching be organized to take account of this fact.

However, in educational theory, advocacy of individual education often derives from moral assumptions. In liberal democratic communities there is a long standing conviction that there exists a moral obligation to minister to individual differences. This ethical concern for individual well-being is rooted in our religious tradition. Since God allows no sparrow to fall to the ground unheeded, the Christian cannot be less concerned with the welfare of any other human being. But as an item of democratic ideology, individualism also derives particularly from the categorical imperative of Kant: 'So act as to treat humanity whether in thine own person or in that of any other, in every case as an end withal, never as means only.'[8] In social and political terms we believe that the individual counts and opposition to totalitarian régimes derives largely from the assumption that these ride rough-shod over the legitimate aspirations of individuals.

THE LIMITATIONS OF INDIVIDUAL EDUCATION

Thus far it has been taken as axiomatic that the cultivation of individuality is educationally desirable. But two reservations must be entered at this point. First, there is the question of how far the development of distinctive dispositions, talents and tastes should be encouraged in schools at the expense of cultural activities for which the learner may initially have little appetite, but a knowledge of which might be considered essential for an educated man. Is there a sense in which care for individual development justifies the prescription of a common curriculum for all children? Is it possible to let a child down by allowing premature or unduly specialized choice of curricular interests and activities? Indeed, how far does the capacity to make informed choices amongst competing interests depend upon familiarity with the wide range of activities which might be pursued in an educational situation? Arguably, specialization ought not to occur before the child has adequate experience of a wide curriculum at the stage when he can think in abstractions and, in particular, before the point where he must begin to make informed choices in terms of the kind of satisfactions he expects to gain from work and life in the adult world. Yet the view that the morality of individualism sanctions a unique curriculum geared to the child's peculiar talents and dispositions could be advanced in justification of the increasingly condemned premature specialization practised in English secondary education. The autonomy of the child's preferences and interests was, indeed, the basis on which the Crowther Committee justified narrow specialization in the sixth form.[9] However, it is arguable that early specialization leads to cultural fragmentation and to a lop-sided personal development which is inimical to that person's bringing a rational and critical intelligence to bear on the business of life. The assumption that educational procedures should be devised which prevent fragmentation into 'two cultures' derives from the belief that an individual is less than his potential self so far as his schooling allows him to pursue one set of cultural activities (for example, the scientific) at the expense of others (for example, the arts).

Against this encouragement to the individual to seek self-realization through educational activities which he chooses himself, there is the tradition which, in Herbart's phrase, believes in the importance of the 'many-sided man': 'The individual grasps rightly what is natural to him but the more he exclusively cultivates himself in this direction the more certainly does he falsify through his habitual frame of mind every other impression'. Herbart's solution to this problem of eccentric individual development was the cultivation of 'many-sided interest'.[10] His ideal was to cultivate receptivity to new ideas from many different areas of human experience. The attack on ignorance should cover a wide front. In this Herbartian view of the individual and his interests, one is more concerned with the quality of living which *might* be realized, than with reinforcement of present interests at the expense of the child's potential for growth in directions of which he is presently unaware. Thus, interest is not a mere motivational device to lubricate the learning situation. It is the *product* of a person's education: interests develop whilst one is being educated, as well as being a point of departure for the educational enterprise.

The doctrine of many-sided interest, far from implying a unique curriculum for each child, insists upon every child learning similar prescribed material. Perhaps a child's interests are ill-served by permitting him to follow his own untutored inclinations. Belief in the intrinsic worth of every individual, in his right to realize his potential as a human being, could lead us to insist upon his following a balanced curriculum in which attention is paid to all those modes of experience – scientific (in relation to both the natural and social environments), historical, aesthetic, moral, religious, craft, linguistic, mathematical – which are sometimes thought to contribute essentially to human development. Moreover, our experiences of the environment are shared with other people. We agree with others about the significance of signs and symbols which acquire similar meaning for those who use them. Against the fact that individuals perceive the environment uniquely and bring distinctive powers and limitations to the business of life, we have to set the knowledge that there are also common experiences which they must learn to understand. The existence of this vast arena of shared experience into which the individual is thrust must give pause to any claim for too idiosyncratic an approach to curriculum construction in the pursuit of individual development. Herbart's approach to this problem of reconciling individual inclination and ability with the need for shared experience was based upon the assumption that 'Every man must have a love for all activities, each must be a virtuoso in one'.[11] The spirit of this is reflected in the practice of those Continental school systems which, even up to university entrance, permit only limited specialization within a wide and balanced curriculum.

Herbart's emphasis upon many-sided interest stemmed from more than a concern that the individual himself might be impoverished by an unbalanced development of his capacities. Narrowness of interest also poses a moral problem: 'where a society is composed of men of widely different modes of thought, each brags of his own individuality, and no one understands his fellows'.[12] That is, the manifestations of individuality may be egocentric and aggressive. Written between the two World Wars, Nunn's defence of individualism as an educational ideal was clearly inspired by fear of totalitarian threats to individual integrity; his was a stand against the concept of the state 'as a super-personal entity in which the single life is but a fugitive element'.[13] So far as régimes built upon totalitarian social philosophies continue to threaten the liberal democracies, respect for the individual should continue to be an educational ideal. It is also possible to detect a dangerous anti-individualism in the society-centred concept of education implicit in the popular cliché that 'education ought to help the individual to fit into his society'. But having acknowledged the sense in which the individual's right to freedom and qualitatively valuable experiences must be asserted against the threat from society, the other side of individualism must not be neglected: that is, the possibility that the individual will gain encouragement to pursue his own selfish aims at the expense of others; self-realization becomes identified merely with self-expression. Strongly developed individuality is not always attractive in other people. Even leaving aside the obvious exception of the uniquely gifted criminal, the ordinary business of life confronts us with people with strongly individual character traits, but with whom one does not wish to associate a moment longer than is necessary.

The classical liberal political philosophers who stressed the virtues of individualism were properly asserting the rights of powerless individuals against the despotism of church or monarchy – historically a necessary and valuable manœuvre. But freed from constraints imposed by these traditional and powerful authorities, the individual citizen may himself become tyrannical, careless of the legitimate needs and interests of other persons. Of itself, the doctrine that the individual knows best, that he must choose and realize his own interests and direct his own life, implies no obligation towards responsibility for other people.[14] In its social implications, individualism is morally neutral. The moral basis of individualism is that men should be free from threatening restrictions upon their persons. It enjoins no obligation towards social responsibility. Considerable indifference to human suffering and want follows from the assumption that social amelioration is only possible through interference with individual human rights.

It is true that exponents of individualism as an educational ideal assume that the 'completely developed' individual will direct his energies altruistically towards the common good. For Nunn, the purpose of educating the individual was that of 'enabling him to make his original contribution to the variegated whole of human life as full and truly characteristic as his nature permits'. However, as frequent contemporary reference to 'the educational rat race' indicates, this ideal is far from being realized. There is widespread concern that education is too often valued as a source of personal affluence and status, rarely as an opportunity to develop talent for the benefit of the community. Even the Crowther Report encouraged this educational one-upmanship when it commended extended courses in the secondary modern school for giving those who took them 'something which the others have not got'.[15] This is not intended as an attack on examinations, vocational education or children staying on in secondary modern schools.[16] But the fact is that whatever humanistic values are implicit in much of the traditional curriculum, the administrative ethos of the school too often encourages individual rivalry at the expense of altruism. Our penchant for publishing examination results as hierarchies or orders of merit aggravates the tendency towards self-centred individualism and militates against the ideals of co-operation and personal service.

It does appear that individual development in the ideal sense envisaged by Nunn requires reference to some moral concept other than that of individual rights. The notion of developing the best that is in an individual requires a correlative insistence upon the individual's obligation towards social responsibility: the claims of social education have to be set against the emphasis upon the child as an individual.

REFERENCES

1   J. DEWEY *Experience and Education*, p. 45. Macmillan, New York, 1952.

2   A. FERRIERE *The Activity School*, p. viii.

3   R. S. PETERS *Authority and Responsibility in Education*, p. 101. Allen & Unwin, London, 1959.

4   T. P. NUNN *Education. Its Data and First Principles*, p. 13. Edward Arnold, London, 1947.

5   For an extended account of the Dalton Plan see H. PARKHURST *Education on the Dalton Plan*, John Bell, London, 1922. A shorter description and evaluation of this system occurs in SIR J. ADAMS *Modern Developments in Educational Practice*, Ch. 3, University of London Press, 1928.

6   Z. P. DIENES *Building up Mathematics*, p. 45. Hutchinson Educational, London, 1960.

7   A. W. ROWE *The Education of the Average Child*. Harrap, London, 1959.

8   I. KANT *The Metaphysics of Ethics*, p. 56. Translated by T. K. Abbot. Longmans, London, 1962.

9   CENTRAL ADVISORY COUNCIL FOR EDUCATION (ENGLAND) *15 to 18* (Crowther Report), Vol. I. H.M.S.O., London, 1960.

10 J. F. HERBART *The Science of Education*, p. 124. Swann Sonnenschein, London, 1897.

11 Ibid., p. 110.

12 Ibid., p. 142.

13 NUNN, op. cit., p. 11.

14 For a discussion of 'possessive individualism' – 'the conception of the individual as essentially the proprietor of his own person or capacities, owing nothing to society for them' – see C. B. MACPHERSON *The Political Theory of Possessive Individualism*, Clarendon Press, Oxford, 1962. In *The Rise of the Novel*, Penguin Books, 1962, IAN WATT also traces the manifestation of aggressive individualism in eighteenth-century fiction and notes its anti-social implications (see especially Chapter 3). MACPHERSON emphasizes the difficulties in reconciling notions of social obligation with the assumptions of a free market economy: 'The individual in a possessive market economy is human in his capacity as a proprietor of his own person; his humanity does depend on his freedom from any but self-interested contractual relations with others . . . The human essence is freedom from any relations other than those a man enters into with a view to his own interest.' (Ch. VI, 1.)

15 Crowther Report, para. 109.

16 I have argued elsewhere that vocational education is a necessary component of education for living, education of the person, etc. See my *Education, Work and Leisure*. Routledge & Kegan Paul, London, 1970.

3: The child and society

In both political and educational theory there is a well established assumption that society stands opposed to the individual; that social education is a threat to individual integrity. In accord with his belief that society was the source of human corruption, Rousseau, the prophet of child-centred education, sought the education of his pupil, Emile, in an environment virtually emptied of social relationships. Thus, it seems a paradox that child-centred educationists have often also emphasized the importance of social education. Dewey[1] once observed that many visitors left his laboratory school convinced that it differed little from other progressive schools in existing 'in order to give complete liberty to individuals' and in being "child-centred" in a way which ignores, or at least makes little of social relationships and responsibilities'. In fact, Dewey believed this school differed from other progressive schools in being 'community-centred'. Indeed, critics of Dewey's emphasis upon social education have argued that the apparently individualistic methods which his visitors observed were adopted for technical rather than ethical reasons, since Dewey believed a particular type of individuality to be a means of achieving a particular kind of society.[2]

Evidently, just as an individual methodology may be used as a means towards educational objectives other than the cultivation of individuality, so may social methods in education be employed for mainly technical reasons (see Introduction, pp. 17–18). If individual tuition is a more effective way of achieving some educational objectives, other educational purposes are unlikely to be furthered without resort to social techniques. This is obviously true of those situations where personal interaction is intrinsic to the activity, as in team games, drama, choral and orchestral music or management training. But social methods are not entirely inappropriate even for teaching those skills – mathematics, for example – which seem also to require individual tuition. In a number of contexts, Piaget has underlined the importance of learning in a social dimension with reference to those skills which can be practised individually: 'In so far as he is egocentric, the child will not trouble to pit his own ideas against those of others, and thus prove what he has come to believe . . . Egocentrism is obedient to the self's good pleasure and not the dictates of impersonal logic. It is also an indirect obstacle, because only the habits of discussion and social life will lead to the logical point of view, and egocentrism is precisely what renders these habits impossible'.[3] Lloyd gives a concrete example: 'It is perhaps sufficient example of the dependence of logical thought on socialization, if we recall sceptical small boys pouring scorn on another small boy, who claims he has trillions of marbles at home. Group discussion soon reduces his trillions to something closer to reality'.[4]

Socialized learning of this kind does not necessarily entail the use of group methods. The process of logicization through socialization might be achieved simply (and more economically) by means of teacher-learner interaction. This, no less than group learning, is a social situation, and more efficient learning might follow from 'bouncing' one's ideas off an experienced adult, than from interaction with one's peers whose adjustment to reality is essentially as naïve as one's own. But advocates of social education do usually have in mind learner interaction with other learners, not merely with a teacher. When Dewey remarked on the anti-social character of the traditional school, he had in mind its tendency to discourage co-operation with other children: 'The non-social character of the traditional school is seen in the fact that it erected silence into one of its prime virtues . . . For one child to help another with his work has become a school crime'.[5] Part of the rationale of project methods derives from the possibility that they permit a pooling of resources, an aggregation of insights, which enriches the individual learner beyond the limits imposed by his own unaided

3

probing of the environment. It may also happen that other learners are more sensitive than are teachers to difficulties encountered in learning. Perhaps there are some problems which one's peers are better able to clarify, and some areas of meaning which can be more effectively exemplified, concretely, by those whose experiences are more akin to one's own than are those of the teacher.

However, as Dewey's formulation of the problem indicates, it is difficult to separate advocacy of social education as a technique – a mere instrumentality – from judgements of value about the moral (not simply the technical) superiority of a social methodology. Prescriptions of social method are often couched in language impregnated with ethical concepts. As well as their confidence in the technical superiority of social methods, advocates of these are often also claiming that they have important by-products in the cultivation of approved social attitudes. And often they are valued as much for this social by-product (the cultivation of sound interpersonal relationships) as for their contribution towards the learning of intellectual or motor skills. Indeed, it sometimes seems a danger that this social by-product may come to be valued above the intellectual skills and concepts which are, ostensibly, the objectives of the learning process. But criticism of Dewey's emphasis upon social education goes deeper than this. Critics have argued that Dewey treads upon dangerous ground in identifying moral experience with social experience. Moral knowledge, he argued,[6] is 'what is learned and employed in an occupation having an aim and involving co-operation with others'. 'Character' intimates 'what one is capable of becoming through association with others in all the offices of life'. And he concluded: 'the moral and the social quality of conduct are, in the last analysis, identified with each other'. This formulation of the relationship between the social and the moral has raised the objection that it obscures the possibility that doing what is right may involve individuals in standing against the wishes of the majority as expressed in law or convention.[7] If we are not careful we become committed to 'the concept of an overall community of interests' in a way which stands in the way of the individual pursuing activities for their own sakes, or disinterestedly seeking for the truth irrespective of the convenience to the community of what is discovered. Emphasizing social education is apt to involve us in making social utility the criterion for activities which schools ought to promote.

These are the kind of considerations which prompt some educationists to contend for the primacy of an 'inner' life against Dewey's stress on the need to refer all experience to what is 'outer'. Hollins quotes Santayana's view that 'In Dewey . . . there is a pervasive, quasi-Hegelian tendency to dissolve the individual into his social functions'; and he comments that this quotation 'attacks Dewey's pre-occupation with the social side of experience; he undervalues the individual's need for a strong inner life of his own'. Hollins[8] has in mind the following passage from *Democracy and Education*: 'the idea of perfecting an "inner" personality is a sure sign of social divisions. What is called "inner" is simply that which does not connect with others – which is not capable of free and full communication. What is called spiritual culture has usually been futile, with something rotten about it, just because it has been conceived as a thing which a man might have internally – and therefore exclusively. What one is as a person is what one is as associated with others, in a free give and take of intercourse'.[9]

It was this passage which G. H. Bantock, Dewey's most persistent English critic, seized upon in the mid-fifties to make his claim that 'the present crusade against "un-American activities" is explicable when associated with the mental climate induced by Deweyism over the last fifty years'.[10] As Hollins put it, Dewey's view 'approaches social conformism which is but a short step to McCarthyism. (This refers, of course, to the activities of the late Senator Joseph McCarthy and not to Eugene McCarthy, contender for the Democratic Presidential nomination in 1968.) Bantock's inference from the final sentence of the above quotation from Dewey is that he believes that 'self only makes sense in terms of other men', the obverse of this being that 'other men only make sense in terms of self', a conclusion which reduces us all to the status of means towards each other's ends.[11] Other people become mere objects to be manipulated for one's own purposes. Bantock is convinced that

Dewey's position denies the possibility of individual autonomy: to assume 'with Dewey that one is what one is to other people' is to imply 'that one has no identity apart from them'. However, this is a somewhat idiosyncratic reading of Dewey and is not the only interpretation which the paragraph will bear. To stress, as he does, the importance of 'connecting with others' and that 'what one is as a person is what one is as associated with others, in a free give and take of intercourse', is to proclaim that part of our humanity lies in bearing each others' burdens. The fundamental Christian imperative 'to love' is meaningless apart from the existence of other persons. This implies a social relationship. No doubt the Christian conception that men are members of one another is capable of being used as a justification of tyranny. But to father McCarthyism upon Dewey is like blaming the Inquisition on Christ.

In fact, Dewey's emphasis upon the primacy of social experience derived from his fear of the aggressive individualism which underpinned American society towards the end of the nineteenth century. He argued: 'Dependence denotes a power rather than a weakness. There is always a danger that increased personal independence will decrease the social capacity of an individual. In making him more self-reliant, it may make him more self-sufficient; it may lead to aloofness and indifference. It often makes an individual so insensitive in his relations to others as to develop an illusion of being really able to stand and act alone – an unnamed form of insanity which is responsible for a large part of the remediable suffering in the world'.[12] Commenting on this passage in a critical chapter which assesses Dewey's share of responsibility for the anti-intellectualism of American education, Hofstadter writes: 'These words are altogether intelligible against the background of nineteenth-century America. The rampant economic individualism that Dewey could see at work in his formative years had created a personal type which was indeed independent, if not to the point of insanity, at least to the point of being anti-social'.[13] (In passing, it is worth noting that putting Dewey thus, in his historical context, is a courtesy which few English critics are prepared to extend to him.) Hofstadter is conceding that Dewey's emphasis upon the social character of morality derived from a recognition of the danger we have already noted in the philosophy of individualism (see Chapter 2): namely, that without some conception of social obligation there is an inevitable tendency towards egocentrism and self-sufficiency (in the pejorative sense of the term), towards the growth of an aggressive individualism. The other side of the tender-minded concept of the sanctity of the individual person is the tougher, aggressive, free enterprise, 'devil take the hindmost', capitalist ethic. Hence the importance in a free enterprise society of a stress upon obligation towards other selves.

There is also another obvious sense in which Dewey was right to stress the social basis of human personality. It is self-evident that, for good or ill, man is a product of his social experience; his early nurture within the family, the influence upon him of teachers, priests, friends and neighbours, the books he has read, the art and music he has experienced, the conversations through which he has tested his beliefs. Culturally, we stand on other people's shoulders and there is an obvious sense in which to be human is to be social. It is either obtuse or dishonest not to recognize the extent to which even the quality of one's inner cultural experience is a social product. Peters has recently exemplified the fact that it is not only committed Marxists who share Marx's conviction that 'It is not the consciousness of man that determines his existence, rather it is his social existence that determines his consciousness'.[14] Dewey was closely associated with the social psychologist G. H. Mead, who also voiced the Marxian conclusion that 'mind presupposes, and is a product of, the social process'.[15] It is true that alongside his emphasis upon the origin of the self in social experience, Mead did recognize that in solitude, the self can provide its own social environment: when the self has arisen 'we can think of a person in solitary confinement for the rest of his life, but who still has himself as a companion, and is able to think and to converse with himself as he had communicated with others'.[16] This conversation with the self may even be preferred to the company of others. But those who argue for the authority of the individual's inner private experience against the pressures

of society are not, presumably, contending that the isolation of
the hermit is preferable to the company of one's fellow men.
Affirming the importance of inner experience usually amounts
simply to the defence of a right to private life. Whilst having
the sort of social obligation enjoined upon them by Dewey,
men also have the right to privacy in face of what are felt to be
novel modern intrusions into this. Especially, we fear the
obtrusiveness of the mass media and bureaucracy. Against these
and other manifestations of the public world we need to stress
the importance of distinctive, personal, private interests and
friendships. We do need to contend for the importance of men
being responsibly concerned with the processes of social engin-
eering and for the obligation upon moral beings to bear each
other's burdens. But equally, we need to safeguard a side of life
against the persuasion towards always and everywhere being
involved with other people. There is room for protest against
the insistence of a tender-minded, radical social philosophy
pressing the individual towards 'total involvement' or 'complete
integration' within a society. Unfortunately, the 'inner–outer',
'public–private', 'individual–social' controversies follow from
our penchant for dichotomizing all educational discussion. The
mistake lies in raising the conception of social obligation and
that of the right to enjoy private relationships and interests to
the level of choice between exclusive alternatives, perhaps an
inevitable consequence of the polemical context in which discussion of social education is often conducted. Common experience suggests that self-fulfilment requires both the cultivation
of areas of private interest and acceptance of social obligation
beyond the circle of one's family and chosen intimates. We do
need to safeguard a side of life against over-involvement with
other people, but insistence on maintaining a private area of
experience can look like the shrugging off of any obligation to
act for the good of other people or to share the burden of human
tragedy.

SOCIAL EDUCATION IN A DEMOCRACY

A further difficulty in discussion of the problem of maintaining individual integrity in the face of social obligation is that we are apt to take totalitarian states as the paradigm of social organization. But socialization in a democratic society poses quite different problems to the educationist. The democratic society is a pluralist conception: the assumption is that associations having widely different (even conflicting) aims and interests should co-exist peacefully, and that individual integrity is guaranteed against the omnipresent State by freedom of association. In a democracy, participation in public life can have something of the exclusive character of private life. For example, a great deal of contemporary discussion about social integration (say of immigrants) ignores the point that what minority groups want (in spite of what they say) is often integration in only a weak or limited sense of the term. They demand the basic human rights and liberties, with as much freedom to preserve a distinctive culture as any other group within the indigenous population. For even without large-scale immigration, Britain was a fundamentally non-integrated society in which people preferred to live and let live in order to pursue a multiplicity of distinctive interests and preoccupations. For all sorts of economic, professional, recreational and social reasons, most of us belong to groups which are exclusive of other people. And this exclusiveness is inherent in a democratic society which eschews totalitarian social obligations. How far this ought to be so is another matter. No doubt the processes of exclusion sometimes work in ways which are morally repugnant. But exclusion is often voluntary: we choose not to participate in many associations and we form groups whose membership is open but which, catering for minority interests, will have little appeal to most of our fellow citizens. And if the insistence upon developing a common culture is a threat to the survival of minority interests and associations, it is important to affirm the values of private life and private association.

Thus, in a democratic society, consensus upon social norms is likely to be confined to agreement that the school should socialize only in the sense of teaching those skills of interpersonal rapport which are the lubricants of social intercourse in any society – politeness, courtesy, tact and those conventions of interpersonal relationship which are pertinent to age, status or sex – and in preaching in a very general way the Christian virtues of tolerance, honesty, charity, veracity and respect for life and property. One writes 'in a general way', since the application of these virtues in the concrete areas of life is a matter of considerable controversy. There are those, for example, for whom there are limits to tolerance, charity and respect for persons; the categories of people to whom they are prepared to apply such values have to be carefully circumscribed. The saving expression, 'Some of my best friends are . . .', is an indication that members of other religions, races, colours and political parties are quite acceptable objects of tolerance, neighbourliness or charity at the personal level, whilst remaining objects of revulsion, persecution, intolerance and even hatred when seen as members of a class. This is most clearly and dramatically underlined in those communities currently in the throes of inter-racial strife. Even where there is *de jure* common citizenship, race is a barrier to making tolerance, charity and justice universal. Professing Christians are sometimes avowedly racialist: South African apartheid claims theological justification. And in multi-racial societies it is probably a majority assumption (especially amongst those who consider themselves racially superior – usually the so-called whites) that the limits of tolerance, charity and neighbourliness have to be drawn so as to exclude some of one's fellow men. Justification for this is sought in the maxim that 'charity begins at home'. In relation to British policy in Rhodesia at the time of U.D.I., the frequent references to 'kith and kin' revealed that the neighbourly virtues are applied only very selectively by many people. There is considerable resistance towards making moral prescriptions universal in the way required by the categorical imperative or the Sermon on the Mount.

In this connexion, it is interesting to recall a passage from an educational essay by D. H. Lawrence (an authority for some critics of social emphases in education[17]): 'Men are not equal, neither are they brothers. They are themselves, and each one is essentially, starrily responsible for himself. Any assumption by one person of responsibility for another person is an interference, and a destructive tyranny. No person is responsible for the *being* of any other person. Each is starrily single, starrily self responsible, not to be blurred or confused . . . Every man must learn to be proud and single and alone, and after that, he will be worth knowing'.[18] It is significant that Lawrence ended this essay with a panegyric on friendship, essentially an ego-centric social relationship. Friendship is not without its obligations. It calls upon tolerance; its foundation is in love. But it is essentially a relationship in which *I* choose, on the basis of mutual interest and affection, the direction and incidence of my social obligation. To that extent it is not disinterested, involving an obligation to charity and fraternity in spite of one's own inclinations. Lawrence appears to reject the notion that social obligation derives merely from the fact of another individual's humanity: one has neither the right nor the obligation to do good. On this view, the social and moral obligation enjoined alike by Christianity and liberal humanism constitutes a tyranny. And in terms of popular reaction to questions of race, homo-sexuality, divorce, penal reform or international relationships, experience suggests that this reflects the majority view of social obligation. Schooling directed towards widening the scope of social obligation in these terms can be justified only on the view that the school ought to be progressive rather than conservative at this level of socialization. In fact, although there is wide-spread support for compulsory religious education, one suspects that this is still acceptable mainly as a means of ameliorating the more aggressive human dispositions; to suggest that children should be asked to take the moral precepts of the New Testa-ment seriously as a basis for social behaviour would be to evoke a much less enthusiastic response.

Even more controversial is the notion that education should be directed towards the removal of obstacles standing in the way of social homogeneity and the cultivation of attitudes towards interpersonal relationships which take no cognizance of differ-ences in class, wealth, status or economic function. There would be many who would favour welfare measures designed to institutionalize the Christian virtue of charity, but only in relief of the more chronic social ills. To concede the immorality of

status or class divisions would be another matter. Yet education
has sometimes been viewed – notably by Dewey – as a means
towards obliterating social stratification. In his view, the values
of traditional schools did not accord with the need for social
mobility which he saw as the essence of democracy. Recently,
the debate in Britain about comprehensive schooling has been
conducted largely with reference to its supposed 'educational'
superiority over segregated secondary schooling; that is, in
terms of its effects upon the intellectual achievements of pupils
as measured by examination results. But the earlier debate
focused almost exclusively upon the assumed social advantages
which would accrue from common schooling, in terms of healing
social tensions by dismantling the class system. The emphasis
was upon the possibility of a common life, a common culture.
However, critics of this advocacy of a common culture argue that
it is essentially tyrannical in its educational implications. It
seems to deny the individual's right to the cultivation of peculiar
talents and excellencies. It frowns upon the cultivation of
minority interests. Bantock argues that the common curriculum
logically implies holding back the able child.[19]

It seems that in so-called Western democracies, the use of the
educational system to engineer an ideal pattern of social
organization is likely to be quite unacceptable. In this democratic
context, the ideal society will be founded upon the concept
of freedom, interpreted negatively as 'freedom from' (see
Chapter 4). The social ideal is that of live and let live. The
fundamental democratic value is freedom of association: no
hindrance should be put in the way of individuals associating for
any purpose which is not clearly immoral. Thus, apart from the
area of non-controversial social lubrication noted above, perhaps
the only agreed social norm we can inculcate is the agreement
to differ. The only commonly accepted social values must be
those like liberty of conscience and freedom of speech and
association which are the grounds for the existence of competing
or exclusive social groups. Differences in political, religious,
class or racial orientation will engender different conceptions of
the good life, of what is morally right or socially expedient.
Many of the interests promoted by different voluntary associa-

tions are incompatible, for instance the conflicting economic interests represented by associations of capital and labour and the exclusive religious and moral interests of different demoninations. The practical consequence of freedom of association is that democratic society is a complex of associations and institutions created and nourished by people with very different value-systems. When discussing educational aims in a democratic context one is inevitably confronted with the question of whose aims ought to be furthered by the educational process. Where 'society' is identical with 'state', as in totalitarian societies, this is not a difficult problem. Because the totalitarian society inhibits freedom of association it is, in principle, free from the educational tensions which a rich associational life creates. But in a democracy, the school is likely to be the focus of pressures from groups with conflicting aims. Families, churches, industry and commerce, politicians, societies for the promotion of all sorts of objectives, the mass-media of various complexions are often attempting to influence the schools, from quite different viewpoints, to promote values in which they have vested interests.

This sort of social configuration, characterized by minimum normative consensus, constitutes both the merit and, for the educationist, the problem of democratic society. The pressures towards social conformity are reduced. But, as opposed to the situation in a totalitarian society, indoctrination in a commonly accepted social or political ethic is impossible in the publicly provided and maintained schools. Parents who wish to have their children indoctrinated must choose private or voluntary religious schools. As the widespread dissatisfaction with the compromise solution to the problem of religious education in 'state' schools indicates, the attempt to square religious teaching with all convictions, and offend none, cannot succeed. In this kind of situation the danger is that discussion in schools of the problems of social obligation will go by default; teachers may be tempted to abdicate responsibility for teaching all but those academic disciplines where there are clear criteria of truth and falsehood. The impression may be fostered in children that in the absence of *agreed* moral and social norms, personal value-systems are neither possible nor desirable.

However, a third choice is possible which avoids both the dangers of normative anarchy and of indoctrination. If in a democratic society we find indoctrination both impossible and undesirable, only social *education* is possible. We seem driven to the conclusion that children should learn to articulate or affirm their own social values. But given the present structure of the curriculum in English schools, this is a complacent conclusion. In the past, social studies have consisted of little more than pamphleteering or sermonizing. They have made little permanent impact upon the learner, perhaps because the 'facts' and principles taught have often borne little relationship to the facts of social experience outside the school. Part of this problem is that any teacher has been thought competent to teach social studies: since everyone has social experience, social education seems merely a matter of describing to children the self-evident facts of daily life. But if we are to avoid both the dangerous extremes of ignorant prejudice and naïve liberalism, it is essential that social studies should be rooted in the social disciplines – ethics, sociology, economics, politics, history, social psychology and anthropology – and taught by teachers having some appreciation of the contribution which the key concepts from these may make towards social understanding.[20] We need a complex of social studies which asks about the nature of social obligation and offers explanations of the ways in which men have visualized and exercised their obligations in different historical and contemporary societies. One cannot pretend that social education of this sort is easy to achieve, but then, education – when properly conceived as initiation into processes of disciplined and principled thought, as opposed to mere factual description of the environment – is never easy. However, given that there are social disciplines – bodies of knowledge and disciplinary processes pertinent to the articulation of social values and principles – social education in a democracy does not pose problems essentially different from those encountered in other disciplinary areas concerned primarily with questions of value, for example, aesthetic education.

It must be an act of faith that such an enterprise will contribute towards 'social literacy' any more satisfactorily than traditional social studies have in the past. What does seem certain is that the teaching of social theory alone will not succeed. Technically, resort to social methodology (see pp. 32–4 above) seems essential, at least to the cultivation of the values and practices of sound inter-personal relationships. 'Learning by doing' seems no less essential to the learning of social skills and attitudes than to the acquisition of motor skills and techniques (see pp. 151–3 below). In this connection, as Dewey emphasized, the quality of the school as a society is all important. It is also essential in a democracy to consider how far common schooling is necessary as a means towards developing the attitude of agreement to differ which, we have suggested, is the fundamental social value in a democracy. How far, for example, ought communities to maintain schools whose expressed aim and intention is divisive? It is at least arguable that in a democratic community where homes, churches, political parties and a multitude of voluntary associations exist to promote cultural diversity, one institution – the school – ought to transcend these divisions in its concern to foster that irreducible minimum of social consensus which is itself the necessary basis of our freedom to differ. Critics of common schools are not slow to point out that even when schooled under one roof, children fragment into all sorts of informal groupings, which displays a preference for social intercourse with children of similar interests, intelligence and class or racial backgrounds. That this will probably happen in a comprehensive school can readily be agreed – but it is beside the point. In the light of our conclusions in this chapter, the root of the matter is not whether children of different backgrounds and interests will mix socially on a voluntary basis (though it would be a bonus if they did), but how far there might be a change of attitude, in the direction of increased tolerance and understanding, as a result of desegregating a school system formerly divided in terms of religion, class or intelligence quotient. What little empirical evidence does exist on this point is not unfavourable to the conclusion that common schooling might contribute towards the development of that measure of cultural unity which is the basis of democratic diversity.[21]

This chapter began by noting the perennial assumption that individual integrity is threatened by insistence upon social obligation. We have argued that in one sense this dilemma is inescapable: as moral beings we cannot escape consideration of the duties and obligations which the misfortunes, follies, weaknesses and tragedies of other people force upon us. But in another sense, the plural character of the democratic society – with its fundamental assumption of freedom of association – helps to resolve the problem of safeguarding the autonomy of individual dispositions and interests whilst satisfying our human desire for the society of our fellow men and our altruistic disposition to promote the welfare of others. In the democratic society, the individual's uniqueness can be maintained, not by withdrawal into a private universe or by aggressive self-assertion, but by the unique pattern of social involvement which a person may choose for himself. Since the forms of association are legion, the permutations upon membership of these are near infinite. Thus, a person's uniqueness is characterized, in part, by the peculiar aggregation of associations and social groupings of which he is a member. A man may preserve his individuality by standing aloof from all association with his fellows: but his integrity will not be destroyed by commitment to a unique pattern of social obligation of his own devising. Indeed, the strength and character of his individuality may well be enhanced by freely chosen public commitment of this sort.

REFERENCES

1   J. DEWEY in *The Thirty Third Yearbook of the National Society for the Study of Education*, Pt II, p. 32.
2   See, for example, G. G. SCHOENCHEN *The Acitivity School*, pp. 82–4. Longmans, London, 1940.
3   J. PIAGET *The Language and Thought of the Child*, pp. 124, 281, 238. Routledge & Kegan Paul, London, 1960.
4   A. LLOYD *Creative Learning*. University of Natal Press, 1953.
5   J. DEWEY *School and Society*, p. 16.
6   J. DEWEY *Democracy and Education*, Ch. 26. Macmillan, New York, 1961.

7 SCHOENCHEN, loc. cit.

8 T. H. B. HOLLINS 'The Problem of Values and John Dewey' in HOLLINS (Ed.) *Aims in Education*. Manchester University Press, 1964.

9 J. DEWEY *Democracy and Education*, p. 122.

10 G. H. BANTOCK 'John Dewey on Education'. *The Cambridge Journal*, Vol. V, No. 9.

11 G. H. BANTOCK *Education in an Industrial Society*, p. 39. Faber & Faber, London, 1963.

12 J. DEWEY *Art as Experience*, p. 194. Minton Balch, New York, 1934.

13 R. HOFSTADTER *Anti-Intellectualism in American Life*, p. 383. Jonathan Cape, London, 1964. See also WATT *The Rise of the Novel*, pp. 44, 91, 92–7.

14 R. S. PETERS 'In Defence of Bingo: A Rejoinder'. *British Journal of Educational Studies*, Vol. XV, No. 2, June 1967.

15 G. H. MEAD *Mind, Self and Society*, p. 244. University of Chicago Press, 1934.

16 Ibid., p. 140.

17 See, for example, G. H. BANTOCK *Freedom and Authority in Education*. Faber & Faber, London, 1952.

18 D. H. LAWRENCE 'The Education of the People' in *Phoenix*, the posthumous papers of D. H. Lawrence. Heinemann, London, 1936.

19 G. H. BANTOCK *Education in an Industrial Society*, p. 24. See also the essays by ANGUS MAUDE and R. R. PEDLEY in the *Black Paper*.

20 N. LEE and H. ENTWISTLE 'Social Studies in the Secondary School Curriculum'. *Times Educational Supplement*, 8 July 1966. See also Chapter 5 below for an illustration of this point with reference to economics.

21 See T. W. G. MILLER *Values in the Comprehensive School*. Educational Monograph. University of Birmingham, 1961. Miller's findings have found some support in a more recent research study: see A. GRIFFIN 'Selective and Non-Selective Secondary Schools: Their Relative Effects on Ability, Attainments and Attitudes' *Research in Education*, No. 1, Manchester University Press, May 1969.

4: The free child

Those who locate the child at the centre of the educational situation usually assert the importance of freedom in schools. They are also apt to be suspicious of authority, necessarily so it seems, since freedom is usually taken to be the antithesis of authority. To justify authority appears to limit the right to freedom. Exercising authority is taken to mean imposing upon the child, making value-judgements on his behalf and ensuring that his behaviour conforms to what adults think is valuable. Some adherents of the child-centred tradition believe that, in the interests of creativity and our need for innovation in a rapidly changing world, the values of adults should not be imposed upon children. Some would even hold that teachers, from a vested interest in maintaining obsolete subject matter in the curriculum, are the last people capable of assessing the implications which changes in the environment have for the work of the school. Hence, their authority is often suspect and against this is asserted the right of the child to freedom as a primary value. But must it be taken for granted that freedom and authority are necessarily incompatible? Can we assert the need for both freedom and authority in education without self-contradiction?

FREEDOM AND CONSTRAINT IN EDUCATION

In everyday speech the word 'free' is commonly followed by one of a number of prepositions: 'from', 'of', 'to', 'for'. These are sometimes grouped according to whether they appear to make freedom a positive or a negative value. Negatively, 'freedom from' suggests an absence of restraint. Freedom 'to', 'of', 'for' seem to imply something positive. They suggest not merely that restraints are absent, but that other conditions are present which stimulate and canalize energy released by the removal of obstacles.

Some recent discussions of freedom have concluded that the concept ought properly to indicate only 'negative liberty' or absence of restraint: 'The fundamental sense of freedom is freedom from chains, from imprisonment, from enslavement by others'.[1] In a distinctively educational context, F. W. Garforth has reached a similar conclusion.[2] He believes that all other uses of freedom, especially its so-called positive sense, are capable of expression in other terms. They are really abbreviated speech forms: ' "Freedom for", is, properly speaking, "freedom from in order to" '. Similarly, ' "freedom of" (for example, of choice) is freedom from with the result that I can choose'. Or, saying one is free *to* do something means that one is free from any impediment which might have stood in the way. Thus, G. H. Bantock, who sees unfortunate implications in this negative emphasis, is right in thinking that the prevailing contemporary social philosophy is based upon the assumption that freedom means 'freedom from'.[3]

Whatever our own personal preferences for negative or positive freedom, it is difficult in liberal-democratic communities to deny the importance of freedom as a primary social value. Educational and political liberals take it as axiomatic that freedom is unquestionably a fundamental human need: 'those who have ever valued liberty for its own sake believed that to be free to choose and not to be chosen for, is an inalienable ingredient in what makes human beings human'.[4] In Kant's terms, freedom is a function of the *categorical imperative*. The right to freedom follows from the nature of man. As a rational being, a man quite simply ought to be free to determine the direction of his own life. Kant wrote of 'the idea of the *dignity* of a rational being, obeying no law but that which he himself also gives'.[5] Thus, as a categorical imperative, freedom is self-evidently a good thing.

However, there are those who would question this presumption in favour of freedom, by no means convinced that we should always opt for freedom and arguing the need for constraints, especially in education. Conscious that in advocating these

4

restraints they are out of sympathy with our predominantly libertarian social philosophy, they often resort to paradox in order to accommodate the notions of both liberty and authority. Thus, we are offered the concept of 'controlled freedom', apparently a contradiction in terms. Or, still more puzzling, there is the notion that one really achieves freedom through imprisonment, as with the insistence of St Paul that to be free one has to become a prisoner to Christ. Bantock appears to subscribe to this view, quoting Donne:

> Take me to you, imprison me, for I
> Except you enthrall me, never shall be free.

But this kind of approach to the problem of freedom in education is essentially a confidence trick. Those who mouth the slogan 'Freedom through Imprisonment' are really attempting to persuade us of the truth of something which is self-contradictory: that *p* is *not-p*; that *freedom* is *not-freedom* but its opposite, restraint. In some odd and peculiar way freedom consists in not being free. This sort of tactic is to be expected from the born authoritarian, but when employed by those whose disposition is towards liberalism it suggests intellectual, if not moral confusion. In justifying his own preference for the negative concept of freedom, Isaiah Berlin has shown the implicit totalitarianism in the positive, freedom through constraint, idea of liberty.[7] He demonstrates the 'sleight of hand' by which restraints are justified in order to engineer the freedom of the 'true' or 'real', or 'higher' self, a tactic frequently employed in defence of the imposition of coercive measures upon individuals, classes or nations. Implicitly, people are often ignorant of the needs of their true selves and of what it really means to be free. Hence, restraints must be imposed and freedom limited until they see the light. Or, more likely, the assumption is that individuals will always lack the insight into what it means to be free; so the 'higher' self becomes 'identified with institutions, churches, nations, races, states, classes, cultures, parties, and with vaguer entities, such as the general will, the "common" good, the enlightened forces of society, the vanguard of the most progressive class'.[8] As we shall see, Bantock does invoke the concept of the 'true "self" ' in his advocacy of men's need to submit to authority.

In discussions of freedom we tend to become trapped in self-contradiction because we can only think of *Freedom*, an abstraction admitting no degrees or distinctions in kind. Men tend to value and enjoy different freedoms and one man's freedom (for example, to drive a motorway through a town) may be another man's tyranny (in being prevented from living in the house where he has happily spent a lifetime). However, newspaper editors are sometimes able to sustain lengthy discussions in their letter columns about which political party is really dedicated to preserving freedom, because their correspondents fail to particularize about freedom. And each party is able to claim that *it* is the party of freedom because it takes the particular freedoms which it champions to be *Freedom* and focuses upon the particular restraints proposed by its opponents as evidence of their dedication to *Tyranny*. But, as soon as we agree to particularize, the way is cleared for considering whether there are not, perhaps, circumstances in which freedom ought to be restricted. There are so many possible freedoms from so many possible constraints that we should never take it for granted that freedom is always desirable and should insist on knowing 'freedom from what?' Discussion of *Freedom*, divorced from a particular context, is pointless unless we are locked in argument with someone wishing to maintain that in all circumstances it is better to be bound than free. Nor does the particularizing of discussion about freedom prevent our agreeing that some restraints are morally unjustifiable or some more onerous than others. To the man incarcerated for life in Parkhurst, every consideration is subservient to the fact that freedom is a single, simply quality and that the small licences he enjoys are not worth calling freedom at all. Again, at stages in the history of subject nations, it is understandable that freedom simply means being rid of foreign domination.

Similarly, much discussion of freedom in education is unproductive because we are unable to escape this notion that freedom is unrelated to particular circumstances. In an educational context where children are habitually denied any initiative or choice and often subjected to repressive and brutal discipline, it is understandable that *Freedom*, pure and simple, should become an educational slogan. Advocacy of *Freedom* for children was, thus, a necessity in relation to most nineteenth-century schools. But today it is rarely a question of whether children are to be given freedom in schools, but of which areas of school life and work are to be freed from what restraints. In what matters do they need freedom and for what purposes do they need sometimes to be restrained? Bantock reminds us that unlimited freedom often becomes intolerable since it confronts us with the necessity of constantly making choices. We need the security of having areas of experience where we are not constantly in a dilemma. But unless we rid ourselves of the omnibus concept of *Freedom* and agree to particularize, agreeing with Bantock opens the door to the conclusion that restraint is always to be preferred to freedom; unless, that is, we have resort once more to the unnecessary freedom-through-constraint paradoxes favoured by some educational literature. The question of the teacher's freedom is similarly a matter of how far he has obligations to fulfil and in what areas of the curriculum he is free to pursue his own interests. Once we free ourselves from this blanket use of the term and accept the obligation to examine carefully the specific circumstances in which it is important to be free and those where it is necessary to impose restraints, we can accept the notion that freedom is properly 'freedom from', without any commitment to anarchy and without having to manufacture paradoxes to account for the fact that some constraints may be necessary and justifiable in schools. Rather than resort to self-contradiction, if we believe that freedom is not always possible or desirable, we should put our cards on the table and contend that freedom may have to be circumscribed for all sorts of reasons. This then puts us under the obligation of rationally justifying restraints and the exercise of authority: we can no longer take refuge in vague metaphysical paradox or emotively charged slogans which attempt to persuade us into the belief that having freedom really consists in its denial. As Berlin puts it: 'to know one's chains for what they are is better than to deck them with flowers . . . otherwise there will be danger of confusion in theory and justification of oppression in practice, in the name of liberty itself'.[9]

Discussion of the justification for educational restrictions upon freedom may be facilitated by the categorization of constraints as *regulatory*, *disciplinary* or *custodial*. Regulatory constraints are those imposed for the establishment of law and order in a community. Disciplinary constraints refer to those limitations upon freedom of action in the fields of scholarship or art imposed by the rules of logic or mathematics, the laws of science or the structures of materials. Custodial restraints would be those imposed upon the immature, supposedly in their best interests.

REGULATORY CONSTRAINTS AND SCHOOL DEMOCRACY

The need for regulatory restraints upon human behaviour seems axiomatic. One is familiar with the person who attempts to cut short any discussion about freedom by asserting that freedom is an illusion, since everyone expects the law to deal with the man who thinks he has the freedom to throw bricks through other people's windows. Some restraints upon freedom seem necessary so that we know exactly where we stand with other people. Otherwise social life would have an intolerably arbitrary character. We avoid suffering the restraints imposed by the violence and passions of our fellow men by giving up the right to do exactly as we please in return for the protection of the law. Locke, generally an advocate of liberty who had no use for authority,[10] put this point as follows: 'Law in its true notion is not so much the limitation as the direction of a free and intelligent agent to his proper interest, and to prescribe no further than is for the general good of those under that law; could they be happier without it, the law as an useless thing would of itself vanish; and that ill deserves the name of confinement which hedges us in only from bogs and precipices. So that, however it may be mistaken, the end of law is, not to abolish or restrain, but to preserve and enlarge freedom. For in all states of created beings capable of laws, where there is no law there is no freedom'.[11] This is to say that a limited surrender of freedom in small and unimportant matters ensures the preservation of larger and more significant areas of freedom in public and private life.

Liberals have usually assumed the necessity of this limited restriction of freedom. The need for regulatory restraints has also usually been taken as axiomatic in schools. Rules are necessary to protect the property of schools and their members, to facilitate safe and easy movement about the school and to ensure a reasonably quiet and orderly atmosphere in which learning can occur: we justify sanctions against the child whose conduct prevents other children from learning. Even an enthusiast for freedom like A. S. Neill draws the line at unregulated child behaviour which threatens the property or the pleasure of other people.[12] However, even this sort of justification for rules in schools is not universally accepted. There are teachers who argue that to make school rules is to be committed to enforcing them, even to punishing misdemeanours. This would involve them in unpleasant personal relationships which they would prefer to avoid. It is odd that this doctrine is often advanced by those who also see the school's primary aim as that of preparing children for life. What does seem reasonable is that rules should be few and sensible, perhaps even that children themselves might share in making and administering school rules. That is, the tyranny of rules is to be avoided by the introduction of democracy.

In the case of mature adults we do at least maintain the fiction that regulatory restraints are self-imposed. Political authorities are assumed to derive their status from the consent of the governed. We deal with the problem of restrictions upon liberty in the interests of social order by reference to concepts like consent, participation, democracy. But even convinced liberals are unsure about the applicability of these principles to the regulation of schools. School democracy is a controversial notion and, as evidenced by practice in most schools, the majority view is probably that children's participation in school government is neither desirable nor possible. However, this conclusion is one that we must certainly reconsider and, possibly, revise. For one thing, the current campaign by students to secure participation in the management of institutions of higher education has already spread into secondary schools. But, more important, it is questionable how far we can pretend to be educating for democracy so long as our efforts in this direction are confined to theoretical teaching in civics of political and social principles which are never exemplified in the schools themselves. In this sense, the question of school democracy is a matter of the sort of moral, social and political education we provide and the way in which we exemplify relevant principles in the life of the school. It is not merely a peripheral consideration of lubricating the machinery of school management in order to minimize the occurrence of anti-social behaviour which would disrupt the proper work of the school. However, even at this purely prudential level concerned with the reduction of friction in the regulation of school life, it is worth considering whether rules might be better understood and observed if children were consulted about them, subject to some limitation on the areas of school management to which democracy can apply. Schools operate within the terms of state and local legislation and of other social expectations which limit even the freedom of teachers themselves, and it is no bad thing for children to learn that all institutions have to operate within this social framework of *given* constraints upon the freedom of action of their members.[13]

DISCIPLINARY CONSTRAINTS IN EDUCATION

The argument for disciplinary constraints (as defined above) is that the subjects of the school curriculum are characterized by principles, rules of procedure and logically related concepts which necessarily impose upon human learning in the pursuit of mastery and the interests of truth. Similarly, creativity in art comes not from unbridled expression but through the disciplined and controlled exploration of materials.

It will be appropriate to explore this problem of justifying disciplinary constraints in school by reference to the arts in education, since it is in connexion with this area of the curriculum that some of the more extreme advocacy of freedom occurs. Those who have advocated complete freedom of artistic expression for the child, focus on the over-riding importance of his own spontaneous creativity and condemn any kind of adult interference in the form of lessons in technique or teachers' value-judgments about works of art. Dewey once critically epitomized this standpoint as follows: 'There is a tendency to say, in effect, let us surround the pupils with certain materials, tools, appliances etc., and then let pupils respond to these things according to their own desires. Above all, let us not suggest any end or plan to the student; let us not suggest to them what they shall do for this is an unwonted trespass upon their sacred intellectual individuality since the essence of such individuality is to set up ends and aims'.[14]

Apart from this assertion that impositions upon the student threaten his integrity, a number of reasons exist for this emphasis upon the child's own free creative activity. Only one of these need be elaborated in this context since it constitutes a major theoretical justification for the emphasis which some educationists place upon freedom in education. The free expressionistic conception of art education derives largely from psychoanalytical theory. The development of depth psychology has inevitably produced a new orientation in our thinking about childhood. Freudians and post-Freudians in education have developed psychoanalytical theories with reference to children's behaviour, and some educationists have interpreted this work as implying that therapeutic activity should be the crux of all work in schools. But these ideas have seemed particularly relevant to the practice of art and art education. It is assumed that there is a therapeutic value in making art and that this is the primary justification for including art in the curriculum.

Thus, at the extreme, theories of art education have stemmed from the notion that the free practice of art alleviates emotional stress. Educational procedures in traditional schools are associated with the bottling up of emotions. What is required is that children should be encouraged to express themselves freely. As Cizek, a founder of the movement towards free expression in art, put it: 'I take off the lid, and other art masters clap the lid on'.[15] Cizek's conception of art as a subconsciously motivated mode of activity – an activity inhibited by conscious intellection –

has points in common with Freud's explanation of artistic activity:

The artist . . . has an introverted disposition and has not far to go to become neurotic. He is one who is urged on by instinctual needs which are too clamourous. He longs to attain honour, power, riches, fame and love of women; but he lacks the means of achieving these gratifications. So like any other with an un-satisfied longing, he turns away from reality and transfers all his interest, and all his libido too, on to the creation of his wishes in the life of phantasy, from which the way might readily lead to neurosis . . . But the way back to reality is found by the artist thus: He is not the only one who has a life of phantasy, from which the way might readily lead to neurosis; the intermediate world of phantasy is sanctioned by general human consent, and every human soul looks to it for comfort and consolation.[16]

Advocates of freedom in education have sometimes been influenced by Freudian conceptions of the relationship between neurosis and a repressive upbringing. For example, A. S. Neill writes: 'unfree education results in life that cannot be lived fully. Such an education almost entirely ignores the *emotions* of life; and because these emotions are dynamic, their lack of opportunity for expression must and does result in cheapness and ugliness and hatefulness'.[17] The writings of Holbrook[18] also demonstrate a belief in the educational value of therapy provided through 'creative writing'. But Holbrook's work also focuses a difficulty which some educationists have with the concept of education as therapy. He has developed his theory and practice of education with reference mainly to 'the rejected' in the lower streams of secondary modern schools and, although he claims that his work has a more general reference,[19] it is open to doubt how far a technique developed in the remedial treatment of exceptional children ought to be widely applied. Critics of mental health as an educational aim, have argued that this is a precondition not the *raison d'être* of educational activity. Indeed, concern with therapy may get in the way of education: 'The chief difference between the clinician and the teacher is that the former is principally concerned with pathology, whereas the latter is principally concerned with normality. For the teacher, pathological behaviour, when it occurs, introduces a disruptive element into his work; something that must be overcome, so to speak, if he is to get on with his proper business. For the therapist, such behaviour is that *raison d'être* of his professional activity.'[20] Similarly, Peters concludes that the mental health aim of education is only convincing on the view that life is 'something merely to be endured like an illness'. To reject this assumption is to conclude that 'the main function of the teacher is to train and instruct; it is not to help and cure'.[21] Against this, it might be claimed that none can be called normal; perhaps even apparently well integrated persons would be healthier if given more encouragement to express themselves. The conception of art as purgation has a long and respectable ancestry. But in Aristotle, its best known exponent, the assumption was that catharsis followed from experiencing the works of artistic genius, not from self-expression.[22]

It is at this point that Holbrook parts company with those whose view of art education embraces only self-expression through the practice of art.[23] He insists on the importance of bringing the young into contact with good art as a means towards maturity.[24] Alongside children's own creative writing must go an attempt to enlarge experience by contact with literature. Control, and not merely the expression of emotion, is his objective and this involves exposure to works of literary merit. Similarly, Dewey's stress upon the importance of spontaneity in education did not lead him to a crudely expressionistic view of art education. For him, 'supposing that the mere giving way to an impulse, native or habitual, constitutes expression' was an error of aesthetic theory: 'emotional discharge is a necessary but not a sufficient condition of expression'.[25] Equally necessary to artistic creation is a wide cultural experience and long periods of gestation: 'fulness of emotion and spontaneity of utterance come only to those who have steeped themselves in experience of objective situations; to those who have long been absorbed in observation of related material and whose imaginations have long been occupied with reconstructing what they see and hear . . . "spontaneity" is the result of long periods of activity, or else it is so empty as not to be an act of expression'.[26]

A rigorous application of this conception of how a work of

art comes to fruition would rule out the possibility of child art altogether. But the educational importance of this standpoint is that it really reinforces the point of view of some of those who are Dewey's sternest critics; namely, that disciplinary constraints are indispensable to creative activity. In particular, G. H. Bantock rests his case for the restriction of freedom upon the assumption that little of value can emerge from spontaneous, unreflective, undisciplined, free expression.

In the creation of works of art it is argued that freedom is an illusion if only because the artist must accept the limitations upon freedom of action imposed by the nature of different materials. The artist is free to ignore the limiting character of his material only at his peril: to work against the grain of stone or wood, for example, might be to destroy the material itself. More than this, it is working with the grain, capitalizing upon the limiting idiosyncrasy of a particular material which produces the work of art: 'There is in all artistic creation a characteristic *tension* between the man and the material in which he works. The artist will not gladly think of his material as wholly passive; it has for him "a kind of life of its own" . . . the artist literally *wrestles* with his material, while it both resists and nourishes his intention'.[27] The inevitability of this sort of constraint would be agreed, by even the most unrelenting advocate of freedom. The disciplinary constraints imposed by 'nature' (including the personal limitations of the artist) are arbitrary and unalterable. On the other hand, some of the inhibiting conditions to which we submit in scholarship or artistic activity are artificial. They are normative, devised by practitioners in the arts and freely accepted rather than inherent in the nature of the universe. This point is well illustrated by a comment of Wordsworth. In his well-known sonnet on the sonnet ('Nuns fret not . . .') he confessed that he had long suffered 'the weight of too much liberty' afforded him by other verse forms. Thus, on occasion, ' 'twas pastime to be bound/Within the sonnet's scanty plot of ground'. Nor was this a cosy retreat from more demanding poetic activity. In his view, the sonnet form was capable of releasing the best of creative energies as the works of Shakespeare, Dante, Milton and others showed.

This point that the limitations and restraints inherent in rules of procedure are necessary conditions for creative activity can also be illustrated by reference to games of skill. It is sometimes argued that rules (for example, the off-side rule in soccer) kill the game. But it would be implausible to argue that Stanley Matthews or George Best would have been better footballers without the rules of Association Football. Unlike less able players, they are not frustrated by the strict application of the off-side rule and their ability to move the ball through the negligible space between a challenging defender and the touch-line would be no advantage if the playing area were not strictly circumscribed. The rules of the game are, indeed, conditions for the flowering of their genius. Rules in games make skilled performance possible and they can be devised to put a premium on skill as against strength, or upon one skill rather than another. The importance of this is seen when, in a mistaken attempt to keep a game moving, there is agreement to forget the rules. To scrap the rules immediately changes the character of the game. As Dewey put it: 'No rules, then no game; different rules, then a different game.'[28] This last phrase of Dewey focuses another important point. It is sometimes claimed that the great artistic innovators (for example, Picasso or Schoenberg) succeed by ignoring the rules, and their example is often cited to justify lack of attention to technique in art education. However, what happens with innovators of this kind is not that they abandon all rules but that they change the rules. Finding existing conventions unproductive, in the sense that the technical problems they pose have been solved and exploited by others, they abandon them but for new ones. To some extent, Picasso, Schoenberg (and Wordsworth in his resort to the sonnet) are playing new games. Without rules or conventions in art there is no communication, just as without rules in a game the spectator finds the activity meaningless. And when some art forms do fail to communicate, this is often because we, the audience, are applying the old rules.

This is an important point, not merely because it reveals the necessity in creative activity of there being *some* restraints, but equally because it reminds us that in order to 'say' something new in art we may need to change the rules. This is the point of democracy: in art no less than in political activity, we need to be able to alter the frame of reference. Whilst some form of restraint may be a necessary condition of creative activity, freedom is still essential to choose one's own constraints: 'I don't like your conventions – I prefer these' is a legitimate and sometimes a necessary attitude for the creative worker. However, whilst teachers may be persuaded to agree, reluctantly, that prudence dictates a measure of democracy in schools in defining acceptable regulatory constraints, there would probably be considerable resistance to any suggestion that matters of curriculum content and method are similarly open to question. Perhaps the adult scholar or artist can be left to choose under what disciplines he will operate, but to be in need of schooling seems, logically, to imply a need for direction in these disciplinary matters. The need for custodial constraints – limitations upon the freedom of the immature in their own best interests – seems inescapable where a person is put to learn (or voluntarily puts himself) in charge of a teacher. The role of the teacher follows from his recognition as an authority who must impose discipline in the interests of sound and efficient learning.

AUTHORITY IN EDUCATION

However, to take this view that the teacher is necessarily an authority poses a problem of justification. By what right does one person assume authority over another and how does one prevent authority degenerating into authoritarianism – the exercise of personal power for its own sake? Authoritarianism has often characterized teachers' relationships with their pupils and this is one reason why the concept of the teacher as an authority is often unacceptable to child-centred educationists.

The danger of authoritarianism seems particularly to threaten the educational relationship when authority is justified in the language of morals. Bantock, who has made a rigorous defence of authority in education, implies that, like freedom, authority can be justified as a categorical imperative: 'It seems to me that the most pressing problem of the moment in education – as in the whole of our social life – is the search for an "authority" that will give strength and meaning to man's free development of himself, that will allow man to come to his true "self", in Lawrence's significance of the term – which, in the last resort is what education implies. That authority cannot be found within the circle of the self, nor can it be found in terms of other selves only.'[29]

In this passage, Bantock seems to suggest that men are under some sort of moral obligation to submit to authority. As some regard freedom as a moral good, an end valued for itself, so Bantock appears to value authority. One hesitates to be emphatic on this point, in view of the ambiguity of Bantock's discussion. For example, it is not clear how or why Lawrence's discovery of authority in the 'inner recesses of man's being'[30] can be construed as an appeal to the 'extra-human authority' implied in the final sentence of the passage quoted. He is also extremely vague about the reasons why people need to resort to authority and there is an absence of any sort of criteria which would help them to identify authority or satisfy themselves about its credentials. How does one recognize an authority when one meets him? Does authority wear jackboots or a mitre or a crown; does it speak Standard English or bark like a sergeant-major; does it write the leading articles in the *Daily Express* or in *The Guardian*; did it go to Oxbridge; does it sit in Parliament or work in Whitehall? Perhaps it does none of these things for Bantock writes of *an* authority and this has totalitarian overtones. His reference to the source of authority being outside the self and of other selves may be taken to imply that this unique authority is God. Whilst there is nothing objectionable about this conclusion, it is difficult to see how it helps us with the problem of authority in education where we are concerned with the authority of another person, the teacher.

It is preferable to begin from the assumption that there is nothing mysterious or metaphysical about the problem of authority. Resort to authority is a fact of life. We defer to authorities in the interests of getting things done efficiently. We appoint referees and umpires to make it possible to get on with the game. When we complain about the referee, we are usually questioning his competence, not his right to be there. Again, we refer to authorities when conscious of our own ignorance or lack of experience. It is sensible to call upon other people when we lack the necessary knowledge or skill to get on with a job. Or we take someone else's word that something is the case when appropriate data is not directly available for our own inspection, or when we lack the intellectual sophistication to follow an argument in a discipline in which we have not been trained. Reference to authority is a condition of the growth of our experience. 'What shall I read?', 'Whom shall I consult?', 'Where is the best place to begin?', 'Have I got this right?' – these are the questions the learner sensibly asks of an authority if he is to begin finding his way in unfamiliar fields. Thus, reference to authority may enhance rather than diminish or impoverish experience. Even authorities consult other authorities for this sort of reason.

However, because it is expedient or profitable to resort to authorities, this is not a moral sanction for authority. And this is precisely the point about authority in contrast with freedom. The justification for authority is not moral, but empirical or technical. In Kantian terms, the need for authority is not justified by the categorical imperative which 'commands a certain conduct immediately, without having as its condition any other purpose to be attained by it'. It is rather a hypothetical imperative, that is, 'not commanded absolutely, but only as a means to another purpose'.[31] We do not justify authority by reference to moral criteria, but in terms of technical considerations: 'If you want to achieve *a*, then you must do *b*'. This means that we don't abdicate to some vague *otherness*; we submit voluntarily to what commend themselves as the superior insights of other people. And we look for appropriate criteria of authority. Authorities are judged by reference to the sort of competence being claimed by the authority in relation to the knowledge, skill or discipline to be acquired by the learner. Authority is identified by asking oneself, 'What is it I want to know?' and it is justified in the form, 'If that is what you want to achieve, proceed in this manner'.

One important consequence of this hypothetical or technical

view of authority is that authority ought to be conceived as a function of persons, not of institutions. We should look for authority in individual teachers, parents, priests, politicians, not in the school, the family, the church, the State, or the party. Yet current discussions of the decline of authority frequently deplore a climate of opinion in which the church, the family and the school have lost their authority. How authority is to be restored to these institutions apart from individual teachers, parents, clergymen and politicians acquiring authority is rarely made explicit. One can concede that there may exist a climate of opinion which could be vaguely described as 'anti-authoritarian' and which makes it more difficult for individuals to establish their authority. But even in this age with the supposed lack of respect for authority there are teachers, politicians, parents, priests who clearly have authority. In this connexion, Peters has drawn a distinction between 'formal' and 'actual' authority.[32] Some role incumbents – the referee, the policeman, the teacher – are set *in* authority as agents of particular social institutions. They derive their right to exercise authority from the *raison d'être* of the institution itself. But not everyone having this formal right to exercise authority is able to do so in a way which would lead us to describe him as *an* authority. As the behaviour of players and crowds on many a football field indicates, it is not sufficient for a referee to have the institutional support of the Football Association as a guarantee of his credibility. Much the same is true of teachers who fail to get a hearing in schools. Teachers cannot expect to have authority *ex officio*; and even if they expect it, the existence of disorderly classrooms demonstrates that in fact they manifestly cannot rely upon the authority rituals of the school.

What gives a person who is set in authority the right to respect as an authority? Actual as distinct from formal authority derives from what a person is and, what is entailed in this, from what he knows. Some individuals, the charismatic leader, have exceptional powers which seem a matter of inheritance. We account for the authority of Christ or Napoleon or St Francis in terms other than their life experience. But when we step down from this level of charismatic leadership, it is more likely that an account of a man's authority will have reference primarily to his biography. That is, he will have had a wide experience of life in general, or of matters relevant to a particular situation in which he exercises authority, and will have profited from this experience. This special experience may owe something to the quality of his intelligence or even to what is usually regarded as a separate quality – common sense. But relevant experience as distinct from innate characteristics certainly does contribute towards authority. Authority may also come from *knowing* in a more conventional, academic sense. The scholar's or the critic's authority comes from familiarity with relevant sources of fact and opinion. Such a person 'has not been put in authority; he does not hold authority according to any system of rules. But because of his training, competence, and success in this sphere, he comes to be regarded as an authority, as having a *right* to make pronouncements. And this right derives from his personal achievements and history in a specific sphere'.[33] Even the referee who, initially, is *set* in authority, gathers actual authority from his grasp of the rules and his competence in interpreting and applying them. To the extent that we all look to others for authority, they must be seen to derive this from knowledge, experience and insight, and not merely from the accident of birth, from superior strength or age or the support of an institution.

To some extent, therefore, authority derives from hard work, from constant effort to keep abreast of developments in one's own specialism, from seeking new experiences and constantly refining the old. A point of some educational importance follows from this belief that authority is a function of personal competence and not merely derived from support of an institution. If we accept the personal account of authority it makes all the difference to the way in which we react to the breakdown of authority. Logically, we cannot call for repressive or coercive measures to re-establish the authority of State, party, family or school. If the breakdown of authority is seen to stem from the failure of authorities to be authoritative, rather than from out-of-hand rejection of authority as such, we must apportion the blame for collapse of authority and, hence, seek the remedy in quite a different place. We cannot simply blame *them*, the rebels, for their stupidity, irresponsibility, ingratitude or lack of discipline. On the contrary, if we are wise we examine ourselves, asking how far the repudiation of our authority follows from a collapse of our own credibility in the sense that our scholarship, insights or techniques are inadequate or irrelevant to the tasks in hand. Neither the formal nor the charismatic conceptions of authority are adequate to the educational situation. Some few teachers may have the charisma of the born leader, but most teachers who actually have authority in the classroom have had to work for it. The authority of most teachers is dependent upon their personal culture and the resources of scholarship and technique which they bring to the classroom. This is not the truism it appears to be. The conclusion that the teacher's authority is a function of his personal education is by no means universally accepted by teachers themselves. For a profession which has a vested interest in promoting the education of others, some teachers show a surprising suspicion of the educated teacher.

The conclusion suggested by our assumption that the justification of authority is primarily a technical matter – in the category of means towards ends – is that a claim to authority must be judged by reference to the sort of competence being claimed by the authority and the knowledge, skill or discipline to be acquired by the learner. Before recognizing and submitting to authority a person must know what he wants to achieve and be able to test what an authority prescribes against the likely consequences of following this advice. In relation to an authority one assumes a posture of doubt, satisfies oneself of his credentials and accepts his conclusions only provisionally.[34] However, the prescription to doubt all authority and satisfy oneself of its credentials can only apply to the adult learner. The advice to doubt everything is of dubious wisdom if commended to the immature learner. The ability to discriminate amongst authorities must be the end, not an accompanying condition of the educational process.

DISCIPLINE AND SELF-DISCIPLINE IN SCHOOL

Another way of putting this would be to say that self-discipline, which child-centred educationists often want to substitute for discipline, is the product of a person's education and not a condition one can assume at the outset. Becoming educated means acquiring self-discipline, amongst other things. When the individual has it he has no more need of a teacher or a school. This is the point at which it is expedient that the teacher goes away. Or, as Peters puts it the other way round, 'For an empiricist a good discipline of learning is one that eventually dispenses with disciples'.[35] Hence, to be still in need of schooling is to be in need of discipline depending on a relationship with another person.

Self-discipline, then, must grow out of a disciplined relationship with a teacher. And educationists who seem to reject the notion of discipline altogether are usually protesting against imposed discipline which never fosters self-discipline. This is a necessary protest since 'discipline' is frequently used in a sense which merely equates it with 'order'. To have poor discipline is to have a disorderly classroom. To be able to 'get discipline' is to know how to persuade (or force) children to sit still and listen. Now, orderly conditions in a classroom are a necessary if not a sufficient condition of discipline. But if one cannot have discipline without order, it is possible and common to have order without discipline. (Generally speaking, that is. The teacher who really has discipline may occasionally have a disorderly classroom, but in the context of the sound relationship he has with the children, it will require only little effort to restore orderly conditions.) An orderly classroom may be a product of threats and punishments, sometimes of a brutal nature.

In education, discipline is often assumed to involve merely a bi-polar relationship. There is the teacher who exercises discipline and there is the child who is disciplined. But the fact that teachers often have to resort to extrinsic disciplinary devices stems, in part, from a failure to recognize that discipline (and certainly self-discipline) cannot merely be the product of a relationship between two people. In the same way, the assumption that discipline is merely a personal relationship creates problems when we attempt to discover exactly how discipline fosters self-discipline. For it cannot merely be a matter at some point (for

example, when the child is old or big enough) of an adult
ceasing to discipline him. Nor is self-discipline the imposition of
self-restraint by an effort of will, exercised *in vacuo*. Some
educationists do, indeed, talk as though it were this. A capacity
for self-discipline is taken to be something you inherit like curly
hair or a high I.Q. It sometimes even seems to be supposed that
a capacity for self-discipline is largely a function of high I.Q.

In fact, the idea of authority being related to knowledge, skill
and experience is suggestive of an approach to the development
of self-discipline. Like authority, discipline depends upon resort
to something more than the mere relationship between two
persons. We ignore the lesson to be learned from history's
classic teacher-disciple relationships (whether in the field of
religion or the arts), namely, that a third element must enter in
to bind teacher and disciple together and to promote discipline of
the self when the teacher has withdrawn. Christ leaves behind a
doctrine as well as his 'Spirit'. The teacher leaves 'a discipline'
in the accepted meaning of 'a subject', a body of knowledge,
skills and attitudes of mind which the learner has mastered in a
way which enables him to conduct himself with authority, but
also with responsibility. He is now self-disciplined in that what
he *knows* constrains him in place of his teacher.

This disciplinary function of knowledge is often overlooked.
Even subject-centred teachers are apt to talk about discipline as
something you 'get' as a necessary preliminary to the communication of subject matter, instead of seeing that ultimately
what you want to communicate is part of the disciplinary relationship. This is what the teacher and learner come together for.
It is a public property which exists independently of each. As we
note below, it is sometimes argued that discipline grows out of
love. So far as this is so, it is the recognition that subject matter
is also a condition of discipline, which is essential to prevent this
idea of the teacher–pupil relationship as a 'love' relationship
from degeneration into mere sentimentality or a dangerous
personal attachment. But above all, having a discipline is the
condition of self-discipline. It is what promotes responsibility
and purpose when the teacher no longer exists to give a sense of
direction to the pupil.

That knowledge exercises this disciplinary function is hard to grasp because sometimes it appears contrary to experience. Like other almost self-evident educational maxims, it seems to break down on the classroom floor. Inexperienced teachers often complain, with justice, that they painstakingly prepare interesting material but simply cannot get a hearing from a class. Surely, then, there is something else which makes for discipline. Are we not driven back to the conclusion that it is something in the personal relationship between teacher and child which characterizes discipline? It may be something which the teacher *does* and the inexperienced, even when they have a moral revulsion from corporal punishment, envy the 'disciplined' classrooms of those who do not spare the rod. But, as we have argued, this produces order, not discipline. As an instrument of discipline it can never be anything more than a first resort. On the other hand, there are those who seem able to charm a class into attention much as Christ was able to compel followers before they grasped or even heard his teaching. Indeed, some outstanding teachers do appear to have something of the charisma of the 'born' leader. But this is no consolation to the average teacher who can merely bring to his work patience and industry, scholarship, humour, a sense of vocation, and, perhaps, a love for children.

However, the teacher who seems lacking in charisma and finds discipline difficult can draw some comfort from the model of Christ's relationship with his followers. Christ himself had less than complete success with his disciples. The twelve included a betrayer, a doubter, two status-seekers and one who, under hostile interrogation, denied all knowledge of his teacher. Frequently they all misunderstood the point of the 'lesson' and only grasped the meaning of their master's teaching after it was finished – when they 'left school' so to speak. It is not surprising that lesser teachers encounter similar, if less dramatic disciplinary problems, or that they spend a great deal of their time being misunderstood. Persistence in the face of these discouragements involves a commitment to children's well-being which some would epitomize as 'love'. But this is a word about whose use we are inclined to be diffident in an educational context. It marks a point to which some teachers are not prepared to go. Whatever else they are expected to do in the classroom, they refuse to entertain the notion that they have any obligation to love those whom they teach.[36]

However, it is not only tender-minded or sentimental educationists who believe in the disciplinary value of love. A teacher of tough children in a London school ended the Preface of his book, in which he promised his readers a down-to-earth analysis of the problem of discipline in place of the vacuous writing which (he believed) usually characterizes discussion of this problem, with the conclusion that the key to the teacher–pupil relationship 'lies in what has become something of a cliché – human love'.[37] It is evident that the 'love' relationships which Farley had developed with his boys was that usually distinguished as *agapé* or *caritas*. In this sense, love lacks the sexuality of *eros* or the familiarity and exclusiveness of *philia*.[38] In the idiom of the New Testament, it denotes a relationship which is disinterested, long-suffering, patient, modest, kindly, seemly, enduring, hopeful, incapable of rebuff or revenge. This kind of relationship was obviously the key to the difficulty disciplinary problems described in other accounts of the secondary modern school.[39] If teachers lack histrionic gifts to compel attention to what they have to teach, their concern for children which is a product of *agapé*, may be a fruitful basis for the disciplinary relationship. Indeed, this might succeed where more dramatic histrionics fail. The 'loving' teacher, in the sense defined, is offering the deprived child something he may conspicuously lack from the other adults he meets. And ultimately, his authority may the better commend itself to the child who responds to altogether different qualities than the histrionics of the 'bright' teacher. His response may be to the teacher who finds something admirable in him: some quality usually disregarded.

However, whilst love may be the key to discipline, it is only instrumental to a relationship which exists for purposes other than the development of personal rapport. Is it fundamental to the character of the teacher–pupil relationship that it must ultimately be dissolved. 'Divorce', rather than prolonged union, is the proper consummation of the successful pupil–teacher encounter. And when the bond is eventually broken, the child must be in a position to stand on his own feet. Ultimately, therefore, something has to substitute for a sound personal relationship between teacher and child. The teacher gives not himself, but the skills, knowledge and attitudes – the discipline – which he mediates. The product of the successful pupil–teacher relationship is a capacity to behave in a disciplined way. If a bond of personal affection endures, this is a bonus. Hence, the teacher's peculiar competence is that of a skilled and scholarly professional, not essentially that of being 'good with children'. The world is full of amiable plumbers, bus conductors and housewives who love children and have 'a way with them'. They are usually highly competent in teaching the disciplines of the home and streets. If the development of personal affection were the primary aim of education, there would be no need for schools except, perhaps, as child-minding establishments during the time when parents are fulfilling their economic functions away from the home. It is the *raison d'être* of the school that skills, forms of knowledge, attitudes and disciplines must be communicated to the young, requiring an expertise which the layman does not possess.

This point is important in relation to the problem of authority in schools. The teacher is not ultimately acting on his own behalf but as one who *knows*, having himself mastered concepts, skills and principles inherent in the discipline into which he initiates the young. He exercises authority as a product of his workmanship, his scholarship, his understanding. And because of this (that is to say, if really under the discipline of his material) he, no less than those he teaches, is under constraint. His judgements are neither arbitrary nor wanton. This is why it is dangerous to pretend, as some educationists do, that the subject matter of education is irrelevant. On the contrary, it is the learner's ultimate safeguard against authoritarian teaching.

Nevertheless, from the child's point of view, the teacher is given. Unlike the mature learner he does not choose what authority he will follow on the basis of his own understanding and experience. So far as the teacher's competence to exercise authority is concerned he has to commend himself to other adults who act on the child's behalf; parents, inspectors, educational administrators and the examiners who licence him to teach. These exercise judgement for the child, using what expertise they have to assess the teacher's competence as an authority. The process of licensing a teacher is some guarantee that he has knowledge, experience and integrity fitting to teach others. Parents (in principle) have a right to choose their child's school, and sometimes they exercise this right arising from what they know of the competence of the staff. (Though it must be recognized that some parents choose schools in which many issues are closed questions, thus exercising their own freedom of choice in a way which limits the child's.) But whilst parents and others may safeguard children against the person who has neither the knowledge nor experience to teach with authority, they cannot altogether exclude the person who may, notwithstanding his qualifications, exercise power arbitrarily, or for personal satisfaction, or whose knowledge is barely adequate or outdated (and there are the competent but lazy who will neglect to refresh their scholarship and exist for a professional lifetime on their capital). Against this misuse of authority, has the child any safeguard?

However diffident about his role as an authority the adult may be, it is a fact that the children he encounters will approach him asking 'why', 'where', 'when', 'what', 'who'?[40] They expect answers, an index of their willingness to rely upon authority. But part of children's safeguard against the misuse of adult authority is that they expect informed, thoughtful, honest answers to the questions they ask. The child is not absolutely trusting. In a sense he knows what he wants from adults. The test of whether their replies are taken as authoritative depends partly on whether the information or explanations they vouchsafe close the gaps in the child's experience. The child's questions are a product of his desire to learn and if the answers he is given patently frustrate this objective, he turns away from person A to person B who seems to be more reliable. At least, this is what happens in the informal learning of daily life when children learn to trust or suspect certain neighbours, relatives, friends or local tradesmen. In the compulsory situation of the classroom where they cannot turn to another adult they become passive, sullen and uninterested, if not positively insolent or rebellious in the face of the untrustworthy teacher. However, one must allow that the child's immaturity makes him particularly vulnerable to the teacher who is not obviously incompetent; who has an air of knowing and a facility with personal relationships, thus masking the obsolescence of his material or his own lack of intellectual rigour. In the end, therefore, if the teacher, apart from his authority *ex officio*, would have the authority which makes for willing disciples and, ultimately, informed and self-disciplined persons, this depends upon his own view of the teacher's responsibilities and obligations and on his morale in carrying them out.

Although 'self-discipline' is not a term often encountered in child-centred educational literature its characteristics are those which are valued by educationists in this tradition: the building of the integrity of the person, the liberation of the intelligence, the cultivation of a sense of responsibility, self-control, the capacity to learn for oneself, reliance upon one's own conclusions – these are the marks of the self-disciplined. The self-disciplined learner is the one who can teach himself, capable of exercising discrimination about those on whom he depends – an authority upon authorities. But these are also the characteristics of the mature learner. Self-discipline marks the end of a process, not its beginning, a factor which is sometimes as much overlooked by those who expect too much initiative and intelligence or too much appetite for freedom from their students at the outset, as of whose who fail to recognize that the end of their exercise of authority is that they should eventually abdicate. Perhaps some of those educationists who emphasize freedom assume too readily that the process of education can, from the beginning, make use of what is really only its end product. Only where the learner is at critical grips with the structure of material can the teacher abdicate with confidence.

REFERENCES

1   I. BERLIN *Four Essays on Liberty*, p. lvi. Oxford University

Press, 1969. See also M. CRANSTON *Freedom – A New Analysis*, Longmans Green, London, 1953.

2   F. W. GARFORTH, 'The Paradox of Freedom' *Studies in Education*, Vol. III, No. 4. University of Hull.

3   G. H. BANTOCK *Freedom and Authority in Education*.

3   BERLIN, op. cit., p. lx.

5   I. KANT *The Metaphysics of Ethics*, p. 63.

6   BANTOCK, op. cit., p. 67.

7   BERLIN, op. cit., pp. xxxvii-lxiii and Ch. III.

8   BERLIN, op. cit., p. xliv.

9   BERLIN, op. cit., p. xxxix.

10 J. LOCKE *An Essay Concerning Human Understanding*, Vol. II, pp. 307–8. Dent, London, 1961. Also *Some Thoughts Concerning Education*, pp. xvii, xlvii, Cambridge University Press, 1902.

11 J. W. GOUGH (Ed.) *Locke's Second Treatise of Civil Government*, p. 29. Blackwell, Oxford, 1956.

12 A. S. NEILL *Summerhill*, pp. 104–5. Penguin Books, 1968.

13 I have examined the case for school democracy at length in *A Concept of Democracy and Its Implications for Education*, M.Ed. thesis, University of Manchester, 1958. See also my chapter 'Educational Theory and the Teaching of Politics' in D. B. HEATER (Ed.) *The Teaching of Politics*, Methuen Educational, London, 1969.

14 Quoted by M. P. POTTER *The Teacher in the New School*, p. 215. World Book Co., New York, 1937.

15 Quoted in W. VIOLA *Child Art*, p. 32. University of London Press, 1942.

16 S. FREUD *Introductory Lectures on Psycho-Analysis*, pp. 314–315. Allen & Unwin, London, 1949. See also FREUD's elaboration of this view of the motivation towards artistic activity in his *Leonardo*, Penguin Books, 1963.

17 NEILL, op. cit., p. 99.

18 D. HOLBROOK *English for Maturity*, Cambridge University Press, 1961; *The Secret Places*, Methuen, London, 1964; *English for the Rejected*, Cambridge Univ. Press, 1964.

19 D. HOLBROOK *The Secret Places*, p. 231.

20 P. W. JACKSON *Life in Classrooms*, p. 170. Holt, Rinehart & Winston, New York, 1968.

21 R. S. PETERS 'Mental Health as an Educational Aim' in HOLLINS (Ed.) *Aims in Education*, p. 85.

22 ARISTOTLE *On the Art of Poetry*, p. 35, Clarendon Press, Oxford, 1920. Also F. COPLESTON *A History of Philosophy*, Vol. I, Pt 2, Ch. 33. Image Books, 1962. And E. F. CARRIT *An Introduction to Aesthetics*, p. 89. Hutchinson's University Library, London (undated).

23 Holbrook rejects psycho-analytic theories which to him see artistic expression as mere discharge. His reference is to Melanie Klein rather than to Freud – or to what he takes to be the popular interpretation of Freud – see *The Secret Places*, pp. 177–8.

24 D. HOLBROOK *The Secret Places*, pp. 38, 135.

25 J. DEWEY *Art as Experience*, p. 61.

26 Ibid., p. 72, and cf. pp. 64–5.

27 M. BLACK 'Education as Art and Discipline' in I. SCHEFFLER *Philosophy and Education*. Allyn & Bacon, Boston, 1958.

28 J. DEWEY *Experience and Education*, pp. 55–6.

29 BANTOCK, op. cit., p. 183.

30 BANTOCK, op. cit., p. 182.

31 KANT, op. cit., pp. 37, 39.

32 R. S. PETERS *Ethics and Education*, Ch. IX. Allen & Unwin, London, 1966.

33 R. S. PETERS *Authority, Responsibility and Education*, p. 17, and cf. p. 27.

34 C. D. HARDIE *Truth and Fallacy in Educational Theory*, pp. 22–3. Cambridge University Press, 1942. Hardie argues the importance of satisfying ourselves about the credentials of authorities to whom we defer and outlines some criteria which authorities must satisfy. See also A. J. AYER *The Problem of Knowledge*, p. 39. Penguin Books, 1956.

35 R. S. PETERS *Authority, Responsibility and Education*, p. 100.

36 Langford prefers to characterize the proper teacher-child relationship as one of affection rather than love: G. LANGFORD *Philosophy and Education*, p. 144. Macmillan, London, 1968.

37 R. FARLEY *Secondary Modern Discipline*. A. & C. Black, London, 1960.

38 See L. A. REID for an extended discussion of the distinction between *agapé*, *eros* and *philia*, in his *Creative Morality*. Allen & Unwin, London, 1937.

39 See, for example, E. BLISHEN *Roaring Boys*; M. CROFTS *Spare the Rod*; E. R. BRAITHWAITE *To Sir With Love*.

40 N. ISAACS 'Children's "Why" Questions', appendix in S. ISAACS *Intellectual Growth in Young Children*. Routledge & Kegan Paul, London, 1930.

5: *The educated child*

Discussion of educational objectives is sometimes prompted by asking what it means to be an educated man. The educated child is a less familiar notion. Whatever account we take of the idiosyncrasies of the individual learner, we find it difficult to escape the conclusion that the child is in school because he is a man in the making, because he is not yet educated. The common view of schooling is that its concern is preparation for a life to be lived in the future, the life of the adult as worker, citizen, parent. Schools are expected to make considerable concessions to the child's future needs and welfare. Parents, politicians and pundits in public life tend to believe that schooling should *prepare* children for life, their expectations varying from vague notions about the desirability of character training to the quite specific requirement that the child should be taught particular skills, especially those related to his future occupation. Sir John Adams once summarized this attitude to schooling as follows: 'Underlying all the popular views of the meaning of education is the belief that it is the preparation for a sphere of life that has not yet been entered. The most common form of this belief is represented in the saying that education is the apprenticeship of life. The implication is that while the young human being is an educand he is not really living. True life lies before him; all his present activity is merely a preparation for what is to come'.[1] Adams went on to name a number of great educational thinkers from the past who subscribed, in differing degrees, to this anticipatory conception of education. Nor is this an outmoded view of the function of the school. A contemporary American educational psychologist with an intimate knowledge of life in classrooms has concluded that the conception of schooling as a preparation for the future is axiomatic: 'From one point of view the school is properly described as a future-oriented institution. Its ultimate concern is with the future well-being of its clientele. A few educators may not like this description and may insist that school is life, and vice versa. But the preparatory function of school is hard to deny even in the earliest grades where the chief goal of education seems to be "enjoy, enjoy".'[2]

Against this future-orientation of schooling, it has been argued that childhood ought not to be regarded in this way as a means, even towards the end of the child's own future happiness. From this point of view there is an intrinsically valuable quality in childhood which makes it reasonable to speak of an educated child. Adults ought to be concerned with the child's capacity for life *as a child*: his attention ought not to be directed constantly away from experiences which have meaning for him in the present, towards the contemplation of those responsibilities, duties, disciplines and constraints which, all too soon, will close in to imprison the adult.

This notion that teachers ought to concentrate their attention on the child as a child owes its most vivid formulation to Rousseau. He conceived the child as a different kind of person from the adult, not merely as an adult 'writ small': 'Childhood has its own way of thinking, seeing, feeling'.[3] And to think in terms of a difference in kind, rather than degree, prevents our viewing childhood as a period of deprivation, an undesirable condition of life which we must hasten to remedy. Quite the contrary. Rousseau's advice to educators was to 'waste time',[4] encouraging them to dwell on those experiences which enrich childhood itself. For in his view there is a maturity for every age which, despite its limitations when viewed from an adult perspective, makes it possible to think of an educated child: 'Every age, every station in life has a perfection, a ripeness of its own. We have often heard the phrase "a grown man"; but we shall consider "a grown child" '. A similar theme was developed by Dewey.[5] He preferred to regard childhood 'intrinsically' rather than 'comparatively', believing it a mistake to think of children as 'candidates' who were merely 'on the waiting list' for recognition as adults. Because our point of reference is 'adulthood as a fixed standard' and our preoccupation is with 'what the child has not, and will not have until he becomes a man', we treat childhood 'simply as privation'. Adams also noted this tendency 'to regard childhood as a thing to be regretted, a period to be abbreviated as much as possible'. He concluded that 'a state of pupilage must not be regarded as a state of suspended animation'.[6] Dewey's remedy for this tendency to devalue childhood was to regard 'each stage in education [as] completely satisfactory to a child in itself. For him at his stage of development, it should be a full life, not a preparation for another stage which is itself a preparation for another and so on, an attempt to reach a goal which continually recedes'.[7]

This protest against preparation as an educational aim is often expressed in ethical terms: the argument that childhood is intrinsically valuable evokes the concept of human rights. As one writer puts it: 'the child has a sacred right of childhood to live in the present'.[8] We noted above that the child-centred movement in education has been historically concurrent with the movement to extend human rights to other categories of exploited persons. But those educationists who made a plea for consideration of the rights and interests of childhood were not merely contending against exploitation of children for economic gain by employers, parents and Dickensian schoolmasters. Their protest was essentially against the sacrifice of childhood in preparing for a child's own future as an adult. A proper respect for children as persons prevents their being regarded as raw material, even for the making of their own manhood. For one thing, we can never be sure that the future to which the present is mortgaged will in fact materialize. In a somewhat melodramatic passage Rousseau made this point as follows: 'If the Reaper Death should cut him off and rob us of our hopes, we need not bewail alike his life and death, we shall not have the added grief that we caused him pain; we will say, "His childhood, at least, was happy; we have robbed him of nothing that nature gave him".'[9] Moreover, Rousseau's phrase, 'rob us of our hopes', points an even more morally dubious aspect of our preoccupation with the child's future. When as adults we focus upon preparation as an educational aim, we can never be certain that it is not our own present ambition, rather than the child's future happiness, to which we are sacrificing his present satisfactions. It is difficult to escape the conclusion that some parents' concern for children's success in school is really concern with their own aspirations. Schools and colleges are full of students striving to fulfil other people's ambitions. The notion of what *we* would like him to be is an interference with the right of an autonomous individual to determine his own ends. Parental concern that children should achieve particular professional and social roles is rarely mere expression of personal preferences which the child can freely ignore. All sorts of subtle psychological pressures and emotional blackmail are implicit in parental aspirations on their children's behalf.

Thus (as with the advocacy that the child should be valued as an individual) there are moral reasons for treating the child as a child rather than as an adult in the making. But other educationists deploy technical rather than moral arguments against our emphasis upon preparation in schools (see pp. 17–18 above). Support from child psychologists can be adduced for the view that it is educationally unsound to ignore the intrinsic developmental needs of early childhood by the imposition of learning situations which require a degree of intellectual development only attained by much older students. For example, it is now widely assumed that the work of Piaget has shown that young children lack certain intellectual structures (the concepts of conservation and reversibility, for example) which makes it pointless to teach them many things from the traditional curriculum, however simplified. (Piaget's developmental stage analysis has been subject to considerable criticism: this has referred to both his conceptual assumptions and his research techniques. From an educationist's point of view, the chief limitation of his work lies in its inference of stages of cognitive development in spontaneous untutored experimental situations. See Chapter 11 below.) His stress upon the concrete-operational stage in the development of intelligence has also been widely interpreted as a prescription to give the young child considerable experience in manipulating physical objects,

as a necessary preliminary to the development of the capacity
for abstract symbolic thought characteristic of the stage of
formal-operational intelligence. This is reminiscent of Rousseau's denunciation of the 'words, words, words' which were
the medium of education in the traditional school and of his
prescription that, since childhood is characterized by 'the sleep
of reason', the child should be subject essentially to the discipline
of things.[10]

However, this Piagetian-inspired stress upon postponing
formal-operational learning is a technical pedagogical point
rather than a moral protest against anticipating adult modes of
thought and experience in schools. The *fact* (if fact it is) of the
young child's undeveloped intellectual structures renders formal-
operational thinking impossible: only on that account is it
undesirable. Similarly, when Dewey called preparation 'a
treacherous ideal',[11] he had in mind a technical or psychological
problem. He argued that the appeal to future benefits and
rewards must necessarily supply insufficient stimulation towards
learning in the present. Since the future lacks urgency for the
child, the impetus to learn is lost when our educational intention
is merely preparation for his future. Thus, on the one hand, we
have teachers concerned for the child's future, convinced that
we need to save time rather than waste it. On the other hand,
we have children 'shilly-shallying', unperturbed by the urgency
of future needs: 'the future prepared for is a long way off [so]
why be in a hurry about getting ready for it.' In this situation,
curriculum material whose relevance lies in the distant future is
unable to quicken interest, and resort must be had to rewards
and punishments: 'external pressure is brought to bear to reach
an external end'.[12] And this is ultimately a recognition by
teachers that the child really does respond to the present more
keenly than to the future: to reward learning and punish error
and lethargy by extrinsic disciplinary devices is only to ack-
knowledge that the future has itself insufficient power to motivate
the child.

A further problem of emphasizing education as a preparation
for the future is that it is likely to be at odds with the first
emphasis of child-centred education which we have already

6

discussed – the injunction to relate the curriculum to the individual child's powers and limitations. If there has been a tre-
mendous gain from acceptance of the idea that chronological age
is no guarantee of readiness or capacity to learn any particular
thing, this benefit is likely to be diminished where we substitute
what Dewey called 'a conventional average standard'[13] for
expectations which are realistically related to the peculiar
powers and limitations of individuals. Yet where our intention
is preparation for the future, we seem inevitably to generalize
both the content of education and the 'amount' to be learned.
Since we cannot begin to predict accurately the future cultural,
political, social, economic or professional circumstances of any
particular child, we must resort to conventional norms of what
a person of even average attainment ought to know of history,
geography, music, literature, civics, mathematics and so on.
And when committed to this conventional average standard it
seems inevitable that we shall deny the development of individual powers which could become the basis of real interests in
the future. Thus, the anti-preparationist maintains that the best
preparation for the future is really to get the best out of the
present, 'extracting at each present time the full meaning of
each present experience', since 'the present merges insensibly
into the future, the future is taken care of'.[14]

But it is exactly because there is this obvious sense in which
we take care of tomorrow by taking care of today, that some
educationists constantly warn of the danger of thus letting the
future take care of itself. One of the most insistent criticisms of
the tradition we are discussing is that its adherents lack any
sense of the direction in which children's growth ought to be
channelled. Inevitably the future will grow out of the present;
but if it is not altogether a matter of indifference what kind of
future emerges, it must, to some extent, govern the kind of
growth we encourage in the present. If we necessarily reap
what we sow, it is important to be aware of what manner of
future we are investing in when we encourage the current
interests and preoccupations of childhood. Or, to put it the
other way round, given that we are not entirely indifferent to
how the future might turn out, what does this necessitate our

doing now? Where a problem arises is in deciding on what grounds adults ought to make calculations of this kind on behalf of children, calculations coloured by their own past experience. The difficulty is partly that just as we can never be quite sure that it is not in pursuit of our own aspirations that we are sacrificing the child's present, neither can we ensure that we are making accurate predictions about the kind of future he will inherit. We lack omniscience, and the old have a nostalgia for what they have known which makes them conservatively inclined in their assessment of the dynamic of change.

A second argument against emphasizing the sovereignty of the child's present interests and preoccupations is that this only reinforces his tendency towards egocentrism from which it is the function of his education to wean him. The immature tend to see their environment (including other people) as a mere appendage to themselves, something existing essentially to minister to their own desires and inclinations. But the wise learn that they must adjust to the imperatives of the universe, not the other way round. Life is a bitter pill which one must learn to swallow uncomplainingly; hence the belief of some teachers in the educational value of drudgery in schools and the justification of curricular activities merely because they are disagreeable. This view, that our education should teach us that life is a disagreeable experience contrasts with the essentially optimistic conception of man and society which characterizes the child-centred tradition. Ultimately, no doubt, this tragic perspective upon experience involves the consciousness of human mortality and the inevitability of death. Yet if this is too morbid a notion to govern our attitudes towards the education of the young,[15] the recognition of personal denial which it implies is a fact of life. At a less fatal level, the tragic view of experience bears the idea that maturity requires acceptance of what must be and that what must be will often be distasteful: 'One of the reasons for calling some people immature is that they are incapable of confronting defeat, tragedy, or unpleasantness of any kind.'[16] Being mature carries the sense of having come to terms with one's limitations, of having come to the realization that the world does not revolve around oneself; that things outside the self, especially other people, are not there to satisfy one's personal whims; that inevitably the universe will not adjust to us so we had better come to terms with an unfriendly environment and develop a sense of our own limitations: 'the feeling of omnipotence gives way to the full appreciation of the force of circumstances.'[17] Bantock has claimed that it is a function of the good school to leave its pupils with a sense of their own limitations.[18] And it is questionable whether this kind of awareness is likely to follow from an exclusive emphasis upon the present powers, needs and interest of the child. Emphasis upon the importance of the child's present happiness, an important item even in the official credo about education, is likely to foster self-satisfaction and to leave the young without any objective criteria for assessing their own powers and limitations.

A third kind of reservation about the prescription that the curriculum should be geared to the child's present preoccupations is that it appears to impose such limitations upon the work of schools that these become redundant. It is not only parents, industrialists and politicians – those who see education as investment in an economic sense – who expect schooling to be future-orientated, but also educationists concerned for the survival of scholarship and cultural values. They are apt to believe that the immediate needs and interests of the child and his own present estimate of what is likely to have future significance are never sufficient criteria for deciding educational content and aims. They believe that it is good and necessary for many things to be taken on trust if anything of enduring value is to be learned. What is externally imposed can 'in good time, take on significance for the growing being, as increasing grasp makes clearer what sort of discipline is involved'.[19] It is important that the learner should trust his teacher: 'follow me and eventually everything will fall into place'. 'Now I see through a glass darkly' is a condition which some educationists find inseparable from the experience of learning in schools.

SCIENTIFIC AND SPONTANEOUS CONCEPT ATTAINMENT

The essence of this last objection to schooling as a present-orientated institution is that the school is concerned with a different kind of learning from that which occurs spasmodically, fortuitously, spontaneously and unplanned in the ordinary business of living outside the school. Developmental psychologists have distinguished between *spontaneous* and *scientific* concepts.[20] Spontaneous concepts, like 'brother', are fashioned out of the intercourse of daily life, elaborated and refined through experience of a variety of brotherly situations in one's own family and the families of friends and acquaintances. Other concepts – parliamentary democracy, China, specific gravity, factorization, the Industrial Revolution, National Income – are less likely to be encountered (or encountered in the necessary variety of contexts) in daily life in a way which makes them intelligible. Spontaneously encountered social relationships are likely to be so numerous and varied that the accurate assimilation of family relational concepts requires little deliberate teaching other than by explanation from parents and other relatives. But 'scientific' concepts[21] such as those we have noted present quite different learning problems. It is not that these are never encountered in conversation in the home, on the street or in the mass-media: the point is that scientific concepts are encountered too rarely or in contexts which do not themselves supply sufficient hint of meaning. The full implication of political concepts like democracy or communism can never be grasped from the context of ordinary usage. The acquisition of scientific concepts of this sort requires a systematic study of appropriate subject areas where usage can be planned to occur frequently and in a variety of contexts such as ordinary living supplies for words like 'brother', 'dog', 'house'. Arguably, the *raison d'être* of the school is that it exists to disseminate deliberately and systematically those experiences of the environment which cannot be had from the ordinary business of living.

This notion that the school exists to foster a scientific structuring of experience suggests a way of resolving the apparently irreducible antithesis between an education conceived as preparation for life and one which emphasizes the autonomy of the child's present needs and interests. For what is usually under attack when schooling is categorized pejoratively as future-orientated is the subject-based curriculum. Yet the subject disciplines do not represent strategies for meeting the needs of adult life as against those of children; they are a means towards elaborating and understanding common daily experience, so that its meaning may be enhanced at any age. The important point about the distinction between spontaneous and scientific concepts is not that they have reference to quite different modes of experience – the former to the daily business of living, the latter only to academic discourse. On the one hand, those concepts acquired spontaneously in everyday life are indispensable to the acquisition of knowledge in its structured disciplined form as, for example, when the word 'brother' and similar relational concepts enter into historical discussion of the legitimacy of a claimant to a throne. On the other hand, it is a mistake to pretend with some critics of the traditional curriculum that the scientific concepts and principles of the academic disciplines have no reference to the business of daily life. Newspapers and television make considerable use of geographical data of the kind which we only learn from geography lessons in school. Indeed, even popular forms of the mass media are replete with allusions requiring some historical, scientific or literary sophistication if any sense is to be made of them. Much the same is true of the content of conversational speech of even the moderately educated adult.

Thus, against those (from either end of the educational spectrum – the subject curriculum tending to be dismissed as irrelevant to the educational needs of a majority of pupils by both progressives and conservatives) who contend that the traditional curriculum represents a 'high culture' whose mastery is largely irrelevant for the average person, there stands the view that the academic disciplines represent a systematic structuring of the common experiences of daily life. As Hirst puts it: 'The various forms of knowledge can be seen in low level development within the common area of our knowledge of the everyday world.'[22] Harré has made a similar point with particular reference to science: 'A study of the working of science must begin with a study of the language of description and explanation. We must begin with the logically simplest kinds of descriptions and explanations – those we formulate in every-day language to deal with everyday situations. In a way the study of the logical gradation from everyday to technical language parallels a study of the historical development of science, for it was out of untechnical descriptions and explana-tions that the technical language of science grew'.[23] From this point of view, the traditional subject curriculum is not (as is often supposed) a device for alienating the school from life, but a means towards a sensitive and intelligent awareness of the nature of human experience and the physical universe: 'by extending and elaborating the use of symbols (which charac-terize the forms of knowledge) and by means of these it has become possible for the personal experience of individuals to become more fully structured, more fully understood . . . authentic disciplines are at one and the same time approxima-tions to the given orders of reality and disclosures of the paths by which persons may come to realize truth in their own being.'[24] A systematic encounter with the subjects of the curri-culum thus becomes an essential requirement of the educated person.

When justification of the academic disciplines is related to this problem of enriching the quality of daily experience of life, the dilemma of whether schooling should be related to the child's present interests or to a distant future adult life becomes unreal. For the young child's spontaneous questions frequently reveal that he has a curiosity about his environment which can only be satisfied by scientific explanations. At the time when he asks his questions he may be quite incapable of understanding the appropriately scientific answers. But the fact of his constant questioning is an insistent demand to acquire those skills and concepts which are not spontaneously given by the environment and which can only be developed by a disciplined acquaintance with a particular field of knowledge. Confronted with adult explanations in response to his questions, the child 'suffers failures and defeats because of the deficiencies of his logic, and these painful experiences create the need to become aware of his concepts".[25] In educational terms this means that far from being merely a means of preparation for his adult future, the academic disciplines assist the child to make sense of his environment as he perceives it in the present. Although adults may appear to inhabit a different conceptual universe, the child's attitude towards this is not one of contemplating an irksome future with distaste. Quite the contrary, he is an insistent petitioner for access to this 'adult' universe.

Any view of human experience which sets the interests of children in stark juxtaposition to those of adults ignores this fact of the considerable community of experience and interest between children and the adults amongst whom they live. Nevertheless, some developmental learning theorists in the Rousseau-Piagetian tradition (that is to say, those who emphasize the *distinctive* nature of childhood) seem fascinated by what the child cannot do.[26] Important similarities between children's and adult behaviour are ignored. Much research on child development teases out the difference and elaborates and emphasizes these as the foundation of learning theory. Popular interest in the work of Piaget, for example, seems obsessed with what are taken to be the negative implications of the lemonade pouring and clay rolling experiments. No doubt it was the limitations imposed by this selective kind of inquiry into child behaviour which Susan Isaacs had in mind when she observed that the Piagetian child is not the 'ordinary child as we know him in his ordinary moments and situations', displaying many of the characteristics of mature intelligence.[27] Vygotsky made a similar point: 'When Piaget says that nothing is more important for effective teaching than a thorough knowledge of spontaneous child thought, he is apparently prompted by the idea that child thought must be known as an enemy, must be known in order to be fought successfully.'[28] In fact, even a pre-school child is learning many things which are keys to his membership of human society and which underline his kinship with the adults amongst whom he lives. And as childhood progresses, children's activities and interests show considerable overlap with those of adults. Thus, taking children as we find them sometimes means giving them credit for a sophistication which we are not always able to recognize. They can, for example, often do more with language than their performance in set textbook exercises (where language is usually made to function in a near cultural vacuum) reveals. As we argue in Chapter 7, affiliating the curriculum with children's lives may make for impoverishment of the curriculum: but it may also provide a growing point more fertile than the materials which come all too readily to teachers' hands. This point is nowhere better illustrated (allowing for satirist's licence) than in a Feiffer cartoon where two schoolboys are in conversation while awaiting the arrival of their teacher. Talking about cars they use words and phrases like 'cam shaft', 'fluid', 'turnover rewipe', 'reorient', 'to compensate for the friction loss by rigging the oil jam'. And when one of the boys observes that he never knew you could correct for skim, his friend replies, 'Well, Mort, that's what school's for. You learn something every day'. At this point the teacher arrives, calls the class to order and asks Morton to read his English assignment. Morton reads: 'LOOK-AT-DICK. DICK-HAS-THE-BALL. TOM-WANTS-THE-BALL. RUN-DICK-RUN . . .'

As well as having the sort of obsessive interest displayed by Mort and his friend in the gadgetry of adult life, in a multitude of ways children's interests are equally those of adults. They watch the same television programmes, play the same games, visit places of cultural interest on family holidays, assume roles (in the sociological sense), have economic relationships, behave in accordance with the laws of physics, show an interest in the past and in distant places, make mathematical calculations and so on.

THE DEVELOPMENTAL CURRICULUM AND THE PRESENT—FUTURE ANTITHESIS

To take an example of only one of these: in administering their pocket money, exchanging objects they value, assuming responsibility for household chores or monitorial duties at school, children learn to behave in accordance with the laws of economics. They make economic choices involving calculations at the margin, which demonstrate an awareness of the principle of diminishing utility and the merits of division of labour. Their 'swapping' activities display an understanding of the relationships between supply, demand, price and the factors making for inflation. Their behaviour implies economic assumptions and a grasp of 'strategic' economic concepts which are essentially those which govern the behaviour of a Chancellor administering the national budget, of firms fixing the prices of goods and communities seeking the benefits of division of labour. Hence, any discussion of whether we ought to teach economics in schools need not begin from the assumption that such an enterprise can only be justified as a preparation for future adult life. Yet this is exactly where discussion of the problems of teaching this and other social disciplines to the average child often does begin. It begins at the wrong end from the assumption that the primary justification of social studies in the curriculum lies in preparing children for adult citizenship. We rarely ask the question whether these disciplines might be fruitful media for helping children to make sense of their social relationships in the present. Thus, in the case of economics, it is assumed that the pedagogical problem confronting the teacher is that of discovering ways of reducing descriptions of things like National Income, Balance of Payments, Budgetary Policy, Prices and Incomes Policy to the language of children. As with other subjects, the necessary simplification of subject matter is thought to involve 'watering down' advanced academic material; reducing to simple descriptions material which is elaborately complex or highly abstract in character. The assumption is that academic disciplines can only exist and be explored at the level of Piagetian formal-operations. However, the problem of simplifying subject matter in order to make it meaningful for children is not essentially a problem of dilution. On the contrary, as we have just observed, fundamental concepts and principles of the academic disciplines are themselves essentially simple. Our approach to the education of the young child should begin by identifying the key concepts and principles in a subject and illustrating these through the simple, concrete, uncomplicated experience of the learner. Arguably, as with the case of economics, the scholarly, abstract pursuit of a discipline is only the application of these key concepts to more complex and unfamiliar data.[29]

This conclusion is in line with Bruner's assumption that 'any subject can be taught effectively in some intellectually honest form to any child at any stage of development', an assumption based on his conviction that 'the basic ideas that lie at the heart of all science and mathematics and the basic themes that give form to life and literature are as simple as they are powerful',[30] these key concepts and principles being intimated even in the behaviour of very young children. In relation to economics which we have used briefly to exemplify the discussion, academic economists have reached similar conclusions about the essential simplicity of fundamental economic concepts.[31]

For Bruner the objective of bringing disciplines to bear on the education of the young is to be achieved by means of the 'spiral' curriculum. This is reminiscent of the long established concentric curriculum in which the learner returns continuously to familiar subject matter. But the notion of the spiral has the additional merit of suggesting repetition at ever higher levels of difficulty and complexity. The circle of fundamental concepts and principles is acquired on the ground floor of education. Development at different stages of schooling is then achieved, not by introducing the learner to distinctively new concepts and principles, but by applying these *first* principles to more difficult and complex material. On the spiral analogy, being educated may be likened to climbing a spiral staircase within an open tower, returning again and again to the same point of view, but ever higher in the spiral with the wider perspective upon experience which this makes possible. Education is thus a matter of beginning with simple key ideas and using these in analysis of materials of increasing difficulty, not of beginning with complex material and asking how it may be diluted to engage the understanding of the young. Therefore, the task facing teachers of the young is not the simplification of abstruse, scholarly subject matter, but rather a development of principled understanding of what is essentially simple and fundamental to human experience. Thus, in the social disciplines – economics, sociology and politics, for example – we are confronted with the task of identifying those aspects of children's behaviour which require explanation in the language of economics or sociology or politics, and not with the problem of reducing explanations of complicated 'adult' institutions into the vocabulary of children.

If we have this sort of developmental conception of human knowledge as a correlate of developmental learning theory we are in sight of resolving the present-future dichotomy in education. Introducing an academic discipline to a child involves both an attempt to explain his current behaviour and experience and the laying of a conceptual foundation for understanding of subsequent experience, either in the daily business of life or in the specialized activity of scholarship. The notion of schooling as the enforced learning of adult preoccupations and interests will persist so long as we refuse to entertain the possibility that the key principles of the academic disciplines find exemplification in the behaviour of even the very young. We require a developmental view of subject matter which neither sacrifices the child's present interests, needs and concerns, nor constantly ascribes to him the role of alien in an adult community. There is no reason to suppose that all subjects of the curriculum might not benefit from a developmental treatment in which the discipline of the concrete-operational stage of learning lays a necessary foundation for formal-operational thought, as well as helping to bring form and coherence to the child's experience in the present.

REFERENCES

1   SIR J. ADAMS *The Evolution of Educational Theory*, p. 63. Macmillan, London, 1912.
2   P. W. JACKSON *Life in Classrooms*, p. 122.
3   J.-J. ROUSSEAU *Emile*, p. 54. Dent, London, 1911.
4   Ibid., pp. 57, 71.
5   J. DEWEY *Democracy and Education*, p. 42.
6   ADAMS, op. cit., p. 64.
7   J. DEWEY *The Thirty Third Yearbook of the National Society for the Study of Education*, Pt. II, p. 172.
8   SCHOENCHEN The Activity School, p. 95.
9   ROUSSEAU, op. cit., p. 126, and cf. p. 42.
10 ROUSSEAU, op. cit., pp. 55–6, 72, 89.

11   J. DEWEY *Experience and Education*, p. 47.

12   J. DEWEY *Democracy and Education*, pp. 55–6.

13   DEWEY, loc. cit.

14   DEWEY, loc. cit.

15   O. H. MOWRER *Learning Theory and the Symbolic Processes*, pp. 416–19. John Wiley, New York, 1960. Mowrer wonders whether learning theorists should 'help us towards a more courageous confrontation with this enigma' (i.e. death).

16   S. I. HAYAKAWA *Language and Thought in Action*, p. 134. Allen & Unwin, London, 1952.

17   W. LIPPMAN *A Preface to Morals*, pp. 176–7. Allen & Unwin, London, 1929.

18   G. H. BANTOCK *Freedom and Authority in Education*, p. 69.

19   G. H. BANTOCK *John Dewey on Education*, p. 550.

20   See, for example, L. S. VYGOTSKY *Thought and Language*, Ch. 6. John Wiley, New York, 1962.

21   Here one is using 'scientific' in a special, but historically familiar sense, referring to any organized body of knowledge: see R. G. COLLINGWOOD *The Principles of Art*, p. 259. Oxford University Press, 1963.

22   P. H. HIRST 'Liberal Education and the Nature of Knowledge' in R. D. ARCHAMBAULT (Ed.) *Philosophical Analysis and Education*. Routledge & Kegan Paul, London, 1965.

23   R. HARRÉ *The Logic of the Sciences*, p. 7. Macmillan, London, 1960.

24   P. H. PHENIX 'The Disciplines as Curriculum Content' in A. H. PASSOW (Ed.) *Curriculum at the Crossroads*, p. 65. Teacher's College Press, New York, 1965.

25   VYGOTSKY, op. cit., p. 88.

26   For example, Flavell's *summary* of the pre-operational period is couched in largely negative terms, though his fuller analysis brings out clearly the positive aspects of development – i.e. in terms of the powers developed at any particular stage. See J. H. FLAVELL *The Developmental Psychology of Jean Piaget*; Van Nostrand, Princeton, 1962.

27   S. ISAACS Review of *The Child's Conception of the World in Mind*, New Series, XL, 1931. Although this criticism is some forty years old and was made in relation to his earlier writings, it still seems the most cogent criticism

of Piaget's work from an educational point of view, since his later work does not altogether come to terms with it.

28 VYGOTSKY, op. cit., p. 85.

29 This argument is more fully developed in my paper 'Educational Theory and the Teaching of Economics' in *Economics*, Autumn 1966. In the same issue of this journal see also A. CLARKE 'The Organic Curriculum: an Experiment in Primary Education' for an excellent account of the teaching of economics in the primary school. K. DUNNING reports a course with similar assumptions for the less able secondary modern child in 'A Developmental Course in Economics for the Average Young Citizen', *Economics*, Vol. 7, Pt III, No. 26.

30 J. BRUNER *The Process of Education*, pp. 12, 33. Harvard University Press, 1963.

31 See: E. DEVONS *Essays in Economics*, Allen & Unwin, London, 1961; L. ROBBINS *An Essay on the Nature and Significance of Economic Science*, Macmillan, London, 1949; R. G. LIPSEY *An Introduction to Positive Economics*, Wiedenfeld & Nicholson, London, 1963.

6: The child and the curriculum

Although the developmental or spiral conception of school subjects helps to resolve the present–future dichotomy in education, some educationists find this approach irrelevant to the problem of curriculum reform. In their view, to attempt to resolve educational dilemmas by reference to the structure of human knowledge is to tackle the problem from the wrong end. An American critic of Bruner is doubtful whether 'a curriculum defined primarily on the structure of academic subjects' would do anything but exacerbate the problem which Whitehead had in mind when he wrote of 'the fatal disconnection of subjects which curses our modern education'. To 'Brunerize' the curriculum seems to be moving the educational centre of gravity away from the learner: 'consider the illustrations which Bruner uses: what factors determine the location of a city? Does the angle of incline determine the course of an inch-worm in climbing over an obstruction? How sound is Turner's thesis on the influence of the frontier on American life? I found not one illustration that seemed to relate to the problem of day-by-day living of ordinary citizens.'[1] The essence of this criticism is that Bruner's are 'academic' questions which ordinary men would rarely be prompted to ask about the universe in which they live. (See pp. 123–4, 210 for discussion of the use of the word 'academic' in educational discourse.) A similar criticism of subject-based courses is implicit in a recent British publication advocating an integrated approach to the teaching of the humanities: 'a frequent cause of failure (that is to say, with the young school-leaver) seems to be that the course is often based on the traditional belief that there is a body of content for each separate subject which every young school-leaver should know. In the least successful courses this body of knowledge is written into the curriculum without any real consideration of the needs of the boys and girls, and without any question of its relevance'.[2] Against this background of continued criticism of the domination of educational theory and practice by 'subject-matter specialists' it is useful to examine the implications of two child–centred axioms: that 'we teach children, not subjects' and that the schooling ought to be related to life (see Chapter 7).

'WE TEACH CHILDREN, NOT SUBJECTS'

Thirty years ago, Sir John Adams reminded his readers that the verb 'to teach' could govern two accusatives. We can teach John and we can teach Latin. We can teach Latin to John. Employing the metaphor of the tandem, Adams noted that there had occurred a reversal of the positions traditionally occupied by child and subject: 'of old, Latin came first, whilst John was kept in the backward region, where, incidentally, he was more accessible to the whip. In these days, John is brought into the position of prominence, and certainly gets his full share of the teacher's attention'. Neither of these alternatives appeared satisfactory to Adams and he substituted a metaphor suggestive of the coach and pair: 'the New Teaching does not put John in front, but drives him and Latin side by side, and one of the characteristic features of the intelligent New Teaching is that the true relations between the pupil and the subject can be clearly recognized'.[3] However, the point of Adams's emphasis has frequently been misunderstood. As one writer comments, 'it has inspired a belief . . . that it is more important for the teacher to study the child than the subject'.[4] Critics have located Adams amongst those educationists attempting to swing the educational pendulum from a subject-centred towards a child-centred emphasis, overlooking his declared intention to encourage the stabilizing of educational practice at a point where both subject and child would figure prominently in the teacher's calculations. Therefore, it is not surprising that Scheffler could recently address himself to this same problem without fear of redundancy. In their determination to keep the Gradgrinds and the McChoakumchilds out of the classroom, some educationists still rally to the slogan which finds no room for Latin (or whatever subject): 'we teach children, not subjects'.

Following Scheffler[5] little remains to be added in criticism of this slogan. His argument is simply that if after a day spent in the classroom, and in response to the question 'What have you been teaching?', you told your questioner, 'Oh, nothing in particular, just children, that's all', he would be as nonplussed as if in reply to his question about what you had for dinner, you answered, 'Oh, nothing, I've just had dinner, but had nothing *for* dinner'. What he would reasonably expect in reply to his question about your teaching would be an answer like, 'mathematics', or 'to be polite', or 'how to play first base'. He would be quite satisfied (at least that you were taking him seriously) if you had to confess that you had forgotten, or couldn't easily describe what you had taught: your 'nothing' might imply 'nothing important', or indicate a disinclination to pursue the matter. Or 'nothing' could mean that you had tried to teach arithmetic or how to swim but that your pupils had not succeeded in learning either of these things. What Scheffler's examples do bring out (one of the practical effects intended by those using the slogan) is that our teaching ought to be of skills and attitudes as well as mere information.

It is important to distinguish our evaluation of the practical effects of an educational slogan from our literal interpretation of it. As Scheffler shows, if taken literally this particular slogan makes no sense. But two practical consequences have followed its popularity. The first, intended by the slogan makers, was 'to direct attention to the child, to relax educational rigidity and formalism, to free the processes of schooling from undue preoccupation with adult standards and outlooks and from mechanical modes of teaching, to encourage increased imagination, sympathy and understanding of the child's world on the part of the teacher',[6] and in the educational context which gave birth to the slogan, success in this intention was urgently needed. On the other hand, whether intended or not, a less desirable consequence has been the creation of a climate of opinion in some schools and teacher-training establishments which has been

7

unsympathetic to scholarship and, in discussions about the education of teachers, has obscured the fact that perhaps we need a different emphasis in their academic education, rather than a diminution of this part of their course in favour of more professional studies or longer teaching practice (see Chapter 10). It is now arguable that even if schools have not been transformed as much as some would wish, the slogan has been eminently successful in creating a more sympathetic attitude towards children in school. But this has been achieved at the cost of diminishing the importance of the skills, traditions, and ideas which have to be communicated in every civilized community. This is why the continued use of this slogan when it has outlived its usefulness is unfortunate. For despite Adams and Scheffler, it is still mouthed by some educationists as though it expressed a profound truth. As a doctrine it is still preached (if only by implication) by some training establishments.[7] And headmasters usually intend the highest commendation when they say of a teacher, 'What I like about Miss Smith is that she teaches children, not subjects'.

If challenged along the lines suggested by Scheffler, those who employ the slogan might object: 'Of course, I know there must be a curriculum, that we must teach the child *something*; but this does not have to be organized into traditional subjects. We must present knowledge *whole* – "you cannot divide the seamless coat of learning". We must integrate the curriculum'. What this objection amounts to is that the slogan would more accurately reflect the child-centred viewpoint if punctuated differently: leave out the comma and hyphenate the last two words. Thus, 'We teach children not–subjects', where 'not–subjects' implies the organization of subject matter on principles other than the traditional (or, indeed, any) subject divisions. What is really being claimed is something like, 'We teach children, not subjects, but human knowledge organized in ways more easily apprehended by the immature or more in accordance with the way in which they use knowledge in their everyday lives. What we want to avoid is knowledge in watertight compartments'. Thus, we are not really involved in a discussion of the child as against subject matter. The problem is rather that of discovering alternative ways of bringing knowledge to the child, given what we know about his development and the reasons why he needs to be educated.

NATURAL OR ARTIFICIAL LEARNING?

The case most often advanced against the subject curriculum is that it fails to take account of the nature of human experience in the world outside the school. It is argued that subject disciplines provide an artificial perspective on to the environment. Whether this constitutes a sound argument against school subjects depends upon how far the word 'artificial' must necessarily carry pejorative overtones. There is a sense in which the categorization of something as 'artificial' is a condemnation of the object or activity in question. Common usage certainly sanctions this evaluative use of the word, where 'artificial' becomes a synonym for 'tawdry', 'bogus', 'affected', 'false', 'unnatural'. In this sense, 'artificial' describes unsuccessful attempts to reproduce something which occurs, aesthetically, more satisfactorily in nature – artificial flowers, for example. Or we speak, critically, of artificial behaviour, as when the Northerner (born and bred) affects a Southern English accent. Artificiality of this sort is jarring: it strikes us as wrong, untrue, unfitting.

However, in a non-evaluative, descriptive sense of the word, to say something is artificial is merely to categorize it as a human creation. In this sense, some of our most valuable experiences are of things which are artificial. The Parthenon is artificial; Bach fugues are artificial; so are the plays of Shakespeare and the novels of D. H. Lawrence; so, too, is the English educational system and Parliamentary democracy; the rules of Association Football and of cricket are artificial – so much so that we think there is nothing strange in altering them from time to time. Indeed, unless by 'natural' activities one has in mind simply things like going unclothed in Eden, tearing raw meat from a carcass with one's teeth, listening only to the music of the wind in the trees, responding aesthetically only to the contours of a hillside and so on, the whole of civilized life is artificial. Not only the tools and weapons of primitive man, but our music and art, our gastronomy, our fashion, our crafts and professions, our games of skill and recreations are all artificial modes of activity, when viewed from the perspective of the Noble Savage.[8] Indeed, it is in failing to cater for this fact that the child is surrounded by a multitude of civilized artefacts that the naturalist plant or growth metaphor beloved of child-centred educationists breaks down. Implicitly, this identifies the teacher with the gardener and the curriculum with the plant's sources of nourishment. But the child's potential for growth may be realized in directions infinitely more varied than are available to the plant. To adapt Gertrude Stein, 'a rose is a rose is a rose' and it is difficult to think of the maturity of one rose in terms significantly different from that of another. But a man is a barrister (or a plumber or whatever) is an amateur photographer is a member of the Liberal party is a 'rugger blue' is a local preacher and so on. Only in a very limited sense are the possibilities of the cultured adult inherent, in the way that the character of the mature plant is substantially given in the seed. No doubt there is a biological dimension to the attitudes and interests we develop: a degree of inherited intelligence is fundamental to becoming a barrister, a kind of inborn physical potential to becoming a 'blue' and a particular sort of temperament to being a Liberal. But in another place and at another time these qualities would be manifest in other activities. Before 1800 or in Borneo, achieving one's potential could not include becoming a professional footballer, T.V. cameraman, Minister for Housing, President of the Junior Chamber of Commerce, aircraft fitter and so on. Men mature in terms of activities which, far from being 'natural' to them, are artificial functions relative to the culture in which they grow.

In being called into existence to nurture children in the civilized arts, the school itself is also an artificial product of civilization: communities create schools because they find it necessary for the young to be deliberately taught the civilized skills and arts which cannot be picked up naturally in the ordinary business of life. As we argued in Chapter 5, it is important to recognize that what school has to offer is not the sort of thing which children naturally or spontaneously learn from daily life. Adults are always confronted with the need to win children over to what must often seem an alien way of life – a civilized way of life. And whilst this seems a natural mode of living to one who has developed the appetite for a civilized culture, it must seem artificial (in the pejorative sense) to someone not having acquired such tastes and dispositions.

If we clear away the notion that artificial learning in schools could ever be avoided by the creation of a 'natural' curriculum, we are then confronted with a different sort of alternative. The choice is not between artificial and natural learning. It is rather a matter of weighing the merits of a curriculum devised from distinctive subjects as against other curricular artefacts. When choosing between one form of curriculum organization or another, we are choosing between alternatives which are *both* artificial. There can be no curriculum which is natural, except in that sense of 'natural' which makes it natural to eat *coq au vin* or Yorkshire pudding, to read Proust or Ian Fleming, to go to church or play Bingo, to play soccer or chess, to save one's money or play the stock market. These are all quite artificial activities in the sense of being a product of human imagination and design rather than part of our inheritance from Nature. But to have been brought up in a certain way makes it possible to say that any one of these activities is a natural thing to do. Indeed, we do talk about this sort of acquired behaviour as 'second nature'. The civilized – the artificial – eventually becomes the natural mode of living.[9]

As an artifice the subject curriculum represents the distinctive ways in which men have learnt to structure and codify their knowledge of themselves and the universe. It represents their attempts to understand both the physical environment and the civilized arts which they have devised for their improvement, entertainment and solace. As we argued above,[10] the distinctive academic disciplines are merely attempts to explore, organize, extend and make explicit what we already know, intuitively, about the common experiences of daily life, as well as providing the instruments of self-discipline whereby we develop our understanding, our interests and our tastes.

THE CURRICULUM AND THE INTEGRITY OF EXPERIENCE

If it is difficult to sustain criticism of the subject curriculum as an artifice by contrast with some form of natural curriculum, how far is it possible to demonstrate its artificiality in the pejorative sense, as something unfitting, inappropriate, untrue to the life experience of the learner? And what are the grounds for asserting that cross-disciplinary or inter-disciplinary or integrated curricular contrivances are educationally more fruitful than studies of the separate disciplines? One important article in the integrationists' creed is that subject studies fail to emphasize the totality of experience: seen through separate disciplines the environment appears fragmentary, incoherent. Knowledge and skill become imprisoned in water-tight compartments: learning remains 'inert' and learners fail to comprehend their environment as a whole. 'Wholeness' is a key word for integrationists. It is argued that subject teaching fails to achieve the education of 'the whole man': by contrast, integrated studies teach us 'to see experience steadily and see it whole'.

In assessing the relative educational values of subject-based and integrated curricula, it is important to examine this concept of wholeness as applied to human experience. Two different interpretations of the word can be distinguished. The first, which the integrationists' slogans seem to imply, is that experience should be all of one piece. Everything one does and knows should hang together with everything else in one's experience. Advocacy of integration is supported by phrases like, 'the ultimate unity of human knowledge'[11] (a phrase possibly capable of sustaining some meaning but usually unexamined in the literature) and 'one ideal bird's eye view of human knowledge'.[12] There is implied some concept of a *total* consciousness or omniscience in which everything a man knows and has experienced sustains him in what he happens to be doing at any one time. And since man lives, thus, all in one piece, his learning ought to be integrated: 'the cloak of learning is a seamless cloak, and we've attempted to unstitch it: the result has been a thing of shreds and patches'.[13] This quotation is a good example of the emotively charged writing which often supports curricular

integration. 'Shreds and patches' are not the only possible outcome of attempts to divide either cloaks or the curriculum:
whether or not analysis or division yields up parts which are fit
for synthesis or re-stitching depends upon the intention behind
the dividing and the sensitivity or violence with which the
separation is undertaken. Moreover, where our concern is with
the diversity of human experience and not, metaphorically, with
mere articles of clothing, there are difficult pedagogical problems associated with attempting to mediate experience as a
whole. As the Newsom Report[14] recognized in advocating a
subject-based rather than an integrated curriculum, learning or
teaching knowledge all in one piece is a very difficult enterprise
and it is odd that this extremely complex approach to learning
should sometimes be thought to be peculiarly appropriate to the
less able learner. Indeed, the surprising thing about a great deal
of curricular development on behalf of 'the Newsom child' is
that it stands upon integrationist assumptions in defiance of
Newsom's own preference for the subject curriculum.

However, the integrationists' case against the subject curriculum does not derive primarily from purely pedagogical
assumptions about the difficulty or ease with which different
kinds of curriculum may be taught and learned. This problem is
secondary to the question of the sort of experience towards
which education is directed. And what really needs to be questioned is this influential, but largely unexamined assumption
about the wholeness of human experience and knowledge implicit in the metaphor of the seamless garment. An alternative
conception of the whole life is that the total or whole of a
person's experience is a sum of quite separate parts. We look
at daily experience from distinctive and constantly shifting
points of view for peculiar professional, domestic or recreational
purposes. Much of what we do and know has little logical or
contingent relationship with other aspects of our knowledge or
activity. What a man knows of Bach has no real connexion with
what he knows of 'cold fronts' and neither with what he knows
of Keynesian economics. No doubt, each of these things has
meaning within a wider context: Bach to his musical understanding and his general interest in the arts; cold-fronts to his interest

in meteorology and, perhaps, to his passion for gardening and cricket; Keynes to his understanding of economics and his commitment to political activity. But it is a mistake to attempt to establish tenuous links between categories of knowledge and experience which really have nothing in common.

Of course, there is a sense in which a person is living all the subjects at once. For example, in listening to a record on the gramophone or watching television he is also having other experiences which form a totality and which can be explained in terms of different sorts of concepts. For example, glancing out of the window he notices that it has just begun to snow. Remembering he has a football fixture tomorrow, he wonders whether it will be thawed by then and reminds himself to look at the late-night weather forecast on television. Suddenly he feels cold and reflects that most of the heat from the open fire is lost up the chimney. Perhaps he ought to invest in central heating, but this tends to disfigure the wallpaper. He begins to think about the problems of heat convection and finds himself in the realm of physics. Or the record is scratched; wondering whether he can afford to replace it (what this would entail going without), he finds himself using economic concepts. But the more he is disposed to think of all these things at once, the less he is getting out of the music or the television programme. Reflection on the wholeness of his experience, exploration of his total environment, has been achieved at the cost of loss of concentration upon a chosen activity. His attention has begun to wander aimlessly and to the extent that for relaxations, entertainment, enjoyment or enlightenment he had chosen to focus upon something he regarded as worthwhile, the quality of his experience is impoverished. Thus we ill-prepare a child to get the best out of his experience if we imply, through the manner in which we organize his curriculum, that whenever he is doing something distinctive he should, at the same time, be conscious of anything and everything else. Something like this seems to be implied by those who argue that most of us go through most of life's experiences with our eyes and ears closed and urge that we must be educated towards a 'total perception' of our environment. But this is merely a recipe for the education of the bore – the man with an eye for detail. What is important is that we teach children to be selective and discriminating in their perceptions, not sensitive to every irrelevant impression which attracts them from their environment. The way to teach children to get the best out of Bach or Conrad is not to do a project on Germany or the sea (though some knowledge of Bach's nationality or Conrad's sea-faring days may be pertinent to understanding them), but to teach them literature or music having some regard to what these are as modes of human experience, the concepts and skills they involve and the child's capacity, at different times, to respond to particular aesthetic experiences.

It is arguable, then, that much of human experiencing has an exclusive and specialized character, its quality, intensity and meaning depending upon our ability, at any time, to call upon particular knowledge and skill and to close our minds to irrelevancies which distract from the business in hand. From this viewpoint, the irrelevant and miseducative curriculum is that which tries to hang together music, mathematics, literature, geography, biology, history and so on. Whatever organizing principle one might use to bind these together would lead to some very odd results. For example, a currently popular focus for curricular integration is the regional or environmental study.[15] This often involves an attempt to bind together the history, geography, art and physical environment of a locality. Yet few regional environments offer similar educational opportunities in all these fields and to put a child's historical, geographical, aesthetic or scientific education at the mercy of what can be learned, contingently, from a particular place would often be to threaten his development as a whole man and to promote the kind of lopsided, unbalanced development against which integrationists appear to be contending. For instance, the geography or natural history of a region may be profuse with exemplar materials which are peculiarly appropriate to educational development at a given age (even, if one is fortunate, throughout a child's educational lifetime). But it may have few literary associations (or none which a school child would appreciate) and the integration of literature into a regional study will often be achieved by resort to works of literature having only tenuous links with the region (a real example comes from an integrated Regional Studies Course where *Gulliver's Travels* was studied because it was discovered that Swift had once spent a night at the local inn), or to the dialect poetry of some local worthy. But the chief educational criterion for discussing a work of literature with children is that it has literary merit and is appropriate to their experience and sensibility. There may, indeed, be a place for a work of literature at more than one educational level. Gulliver may be taught as a 'fairy story' or as a political satire. But at the one level we would judge it appropriate because children need fairy stories or tales of romance and adventure, at the other because we judge them ready for satire: but in neither case because of the purely fortuitous geographical meanderings of Dean Swift.

Examples of the way in which particular environments would throw up an unbalanced education could be multiplied. A large industrial city like Manchester will be in the mainstream of a great deal of historical development especially of the history of industrialism. By stretching the imagination one might even find there examples of all the major phases of national history. But, by contrast, it has associations with few major figures in the arts. An aesthetic education located in the Arts of Manchester would lead anyone into a condition of acute cultural deprivation. On the other hand, localities having rich literary associations might offer nothing historically more significant than the story of the parish pump. One enthusiastic advocate[16] of an integrated environmental studies course devised for a rural locality does recognize this problem of the environment which is richly endowed by nature but lacking in the culture of an urban situation. She realizes 'that though the district in which our college is situated is admirable for a study of the natural environment in general, and Geology, Geomorphology and Ecology in particular, our very strengths could be our weakness in the concept of an integrated course drawing upon relevant aspects of Biology, Geography, English and History supported by Sociology, Outdoor Pursuits and Creative Work'. This 'could lead on the one hand to the overweighting of subjects that were catered for more generously by the very nature of the district, and on the other hand to the "dragging in" of at least irrelevant and at worst unworthy material in the less well-endowed subjects'. But nothing is said about resolving this problem except in the tautology: 'Since it is an integrated course difficulties of balance between the disciplines have already been resolved'. That is, by definition, integration rules out the possibility that a course could be unbalanced in its neglect of important areas of experience.

As a form of integrated curriculum the regional study seems peculiarly vulnerable to the danger of developing cultural parochialism. The integrity of the environment may be preserved but at a culturally barren level. It should be emphasized, however, that one is not attacking the suggestion that the local environment should be studied as a necessary part of a child's education. What is questioned is the notion that the region should be studied exclusively, at the expense of subject disciplines, on the grounds that subjects can only be properly understood when integrated within local studies. However, it is difficult to conceive of any integrating principle which, by itself, does proper justice to the cultural possibilities of the universe.[17] Our discussion suggests that any integrated project study is likely to have two major pedagogical shortcomings. First, it is likely to project the learner into a particular subject area at the wrong disciplinary level. In terms of the learning process, the organization of subject matter for the purposes of integration often frustrates the order of priority required for sound developmental learning. The earlier example of the problem of readiness for *Gulliver's Travels* is a case in point. Or an industrial town might exemplify all the important points to be made about urban geography, yet be quite an unsuitable environment for the geographical education of the young child.[18] Or again, we may be involved in solving a problem thrown up by a project which requires application of a mathematical principle of some complexity. Yet the children may be ignorant of the simpler mathematical elements and processes which it entails. At this point the teacher faces a dilemma. Does he break free of the project, holding up its development whilst all the necessarily antecedent mathematical processes are learned, even supposing the children are competent to grasp these? Or does he offer them a rule of thumb and ask them to take things on trust? In this connexion it is interesting that one rarely encounters the suggestion that mathematics should be entirely integrated within an integrated studies course. This fate (that is to say, loss of a separate identity within the curriculum) is usually reserved for history, geography, literature and the social disciplines. The implication is that these are 'frills' which we could well manage without, but the ability to calculate is a skill so indispensable to the conduct of life that its mastery cannot be guaranteed through the fortuitous occasions on which mathematics might enter into an integrated topic. The need for 'sequential learning', or 'methodological teaching'[19] is usually invoked to pull maths (and sometimes language teaching) out of the integrated curriculum. At most it is usually claimed that topics or projects provide opportunities for applying or developing mathematical skills which have been learned separately in mathematics lessons. Yet, if a proper grasp of mathematics depends upon careful structuring of the maths syllabus to match children's developing cognitive powers and to cater for the epistemological priorities involved in learning mathematics, why should it be supposed that understanding or mastering other subjects does not require teaching with the same careful attention to the relationship between facts, concepts and principles and the necessary antecedence of any of these to any other? In mathematics subtraction presupposes addition, the solution of quadratic equations requires a knowledge of factorization, the theorem of Pythagoras, a familiarity with geometrical shapes (the congruency of triangles; the square as both an arithmetical and an algebraic concept) and square roots. But in a subject like history there is also the question of what concepts are assumed in what one is trying to teach. How far must there be an understanding of words like pilgrimage, dynasty, century, treaty, law, tax, where these figure prominently and centrally in historical description? Or is an ability to categorize persons as kings, presidents, ministers, rebels, serfs, monks etc. assumed? Or the antecedent knowledge may be drawn from another subject as is often the case in the study of geography. Thus it

is not only in mathematics that repetition, even drill, is required
for mastery of skills and concepts. With reference to any subject
the incidental approach through integrated project studies may
offer insufficient satisfactory incidents either to exemplify the
range and complexity of human experience and natural phenomena, or for the proper mastery of the concepts or principles to
which the children are being introduced. In his classical example
of a project study which would embrace all areas of knowledge,
Dewey was stretching his imagination and his readers' credulity
somewhat, when he argued that 'you can concentrate the history
of all mankind into the evolution of the flax, cotton and wool
fibres into clothing'.[20] One can be satisfied with the lopsided
view of human knowledge which must often develop from the
integrated curriculum, only if one takes the view that it does not
matter much what is taught as long as children learn something:
'We teach children, not subjects.' With this sort of curricular
device one can only conclude that one is driven into as much
artificiality (in the pejorative sense) as was ever the case with a
subject curriculum.

However, to emphasize the specialized and isolated character
of much human experience is clearly not to say everything about
it. The notion of 'seeing experience whole' is an important
concept in relation to those life experiences which do require
insights from diverse aspects of human knowledge. Undoubtedly
we do have the sort of specialized interest – in music, literature,
gardening, golf, medicine, carpentry etc. – which we noted
above; but we are also involved in human activities which cut
across, or gather together, interests of this kind. Many aspects
of social policy need to be approached from several points of
view. The problem of housing, for example, has economic,
sociological, moral, aesthetic, legal, medical (health), technological and historic dimensions. Much the same is true of
problems affecting race, the mass media, poverty and so on.
Whilst recognizing the necessity for giving consideration of
these issues a place in the curriculum, there is also a danger in
focusing upon social problems when this approach is combined
with advocacy of education through problem solving. The
notion that solutions to problems which have eluded entire

communities (sometimes for centuries) may lie within the grasp of fifteen-year-old leavers – especially those less able learners for whom integrated social studies are often prescribed – is dangerous. Perhaps when we integrate the curriculum around social problems, the real justification for this is not that we are synthesizing the insights from separate disciplines into *solutions* but, at the level of social understanding, we teach children to approach social problems from a number of different angles and to see experience from as many relevant facets as possible, so that they resist prejudiced conclusions or simple solutions.

SUBJECTS AND INTEGRATED STUDIES

However, acquiring this capacity for synthesizing our insights does not require the complete abandonment of the subject for the integrated curriculum. It is arguable that synthesis – putting together – requires a knowledge of the separate parts which are to be integrated into a whole. The multi-dimensional character of some human problems can only be evident to those aware of the separate dimensions which contribute to the complexity of the problem. To take account of the complex issues involved in the problem of housing is to know that this is a complicated problem and to understand the sort of contribution which different kinds of specialist can make. It is only possible to integrate into a 'whole', things of whose existence one is already aware. Those who aspire to integrate materials from different fields of knowledge must know that these exist and the kinds of data with which they deal.

It becomes apparent that subject disciplines and integrated project studies are not curricular alternatives. Their educational functions are complementary rather than exclusive: each contributes different but essential learning experiences within a person's education. Integrated studies seem a poor instrument for acquiring knowledge and skill in a manageable, disciplined form. Their value lies in the experience they provide of learning to understand problems which fall outside or across distinctive disciplines. However, an education which aims at *mastery* of skills, concepts or principles must pay proper attention to the epistemological priorities and sequences involved in learning them. To this end, subject matter organized in distinctive disciplinary areas seems educationally superior to integrated studies. But it is only through the educationist's propensity to dichotomize educational problems that we seem driven towards making an exclusive choice between the subject-based and the integrated curriculum. On a rhythmic view of education as outlined by Whitehead (see Appendix), there is room for both approaches to curriculum development. Each embraces disciplines and skills which have peculiar educational values. In Whitehead's terminology integrated studies can be seen as a stage of *generalization* following the *precision* learning of subjects. So far as the subtlest possible diagnosis of a problem may depend upon existing familiarity with diverse fields of knowledge and skill, it would seem, logically, that integrated courses should *follow* the learning of subjects. An integrated course of study is a poor instrument for achieving some educational objectives, but it is important to distinguish between integration as an unsatisfactory mode of acquiring disciplined knowledge and skill, and integrated project situations as providing opportunities to generalize or use skill and knowledge which has already been mastered.

Whitehead's terminology also suggests another important sense in which the motivation towards precision study of a discipline may come from outside the subject itself. His stage of precision had to develop from a *romance* stage of learning. And a problem from 'real' life, or some extra-curricular school activity, or even another subject, may function as romance, stimulating the learner to come to grips with the 'grammar' of the subject. It is sometimes evident that children are driven to study what they might otherwise find uncongenial because they discover it in the process of learning something else. To take an actual example from school life: some children wrote a radio script depicting an historical event; wishing to supply background music they turned naturally to the popular music with which they were familiar and which they enjoyed. But immediately they recognized this to be unsuitable. There was incongruity between the levity of the music and the gravity and dignity of the event to be illustrated. They recalled that there are other sorts of music: there was consultation with the music teacher and his suggestions were tried and found appropriate to the occasion. Thus, these children discovered 'serious' music through a learning experience which, initially, was non-musical. This sort of fortuitous 'discovery' learning is sometimes used to justify adoption of an integrated curriculum. It is argued that when subjects are locked in watertight compartments this kind of valuable cross-fertilization and development of novel interests rarely occurs. But discovery of an interest is not the same as mastery, and mastery is only likely to be achieved when children's musical education breaks free from the contingencies of history (or whatever subject or situation to which its discovery is incidental) and musical terms, concepts and techniques are mastered through the disciplined study of music itself. Musical incidents in other curricular areas are encountered too haphazardly for us to leave a child's musical development to that sort of chance encounter. The education of musical taste requires a precision study of music. But this is not to say that as a romance device, a good teacher of music might not contrive situations in which novel musical encounters arise out of another curricular area or extra–curricular activity.

CURRICULAR INTEGRATION THROUGH SUBJECT STUDIES

This example also suggests the possibility of pursuing integration of knowledge and experience through the subject curriculum itself. We can teach subjects 'project-wise', that is, conscious of their connectedness with other subject areas and using every opportunity to illustrate disciplinary principles with concrete examples from life outside the school of current concern or of particular interest to the learner. The subject teacher needs to be sensitive to areas of overlap between his discipline and others. It is impossible to teach a great deal of history without reference to geography. Some geographical phenomena (the economic activity of New England, for example) are inexplicable apart from reference to their historical aspect. Science, art and music all have an historical context. The necessary antecedent knowledge upon which we build in many subjects lies within other disciplines. Again, the teaching of particular subjects affords many opportunities to illuminate social issues confronting the community outside the school. The teacher of English colonial history (and this is substantially what English history over the last four hundred years consists of) might well raise the question of how far the problems of multi-racialism (and, consequently, a great deal of racial tension) in Rhodesia, South Africa and North America is a product of English imperialism over the centuries. For example, the seventeenth-century 'trade triangle' – in which 'baubles' were taken from England to Africa, exchanged for Negroes, who in turn were sold in the New World as slaves in payment for sugar which was brought back to England – is more than a description of a remote event with its own intrinsically historical causes. It is also a reason why there is today a substantial negro population in the U.S.A. with all that follows from this in contemporary American society. The purist will retort that history only throws light on the past and is misused when employed practically as a means towards understanding the present. Nevertheless, one of the valuable insights which the non-specialist derives from a study of history is the realization that 'the world was not born yesterday', that most contemporary social problems have their roots in the past, failure to understand this being a frequent cause of our inability to devise appropriate measures for social amelioration and reform. However much philosophers of history may contend that the specialist historian should lock himself up in the past, it is obtuse or perverse of them to want to deny whatever practical insights we might find in the story the historian tells.[21] R. S. Peters has coined the term 'cognitive overspill' to categorize those insights which may follow, contingently, from the scholarly study of a discipline. As he himself suggests, there is something wrong with his education when a man fails 'to connect his knowledge of the Industrial Revolution with what he sees when visiting Manchester or a Welsh Valley. We might describe such a man as "knowledgeable" but we would never describe him as "educated"; for "education" implies that a man's outlook is transformed by what he knows'.[22] Even Dewey, who is usually

8

thought of as an advocate of integrated project studies rather than the teaching of distinctive subjects, made the point that the subject lesson could help to transform a person's outlook in this way: 'Every recitation in every subject gives an opportunity for establishing cross connections between the subject matter of the lesson and the wider and more direct experiences of everyday life'.[23]

This suggests the importance of learning a discipline within a context of specifically related knowledge, rather than in relation to knowledge as a whole. *Context* rather than *wholeness* is the helpful conception. Whitehead's prescription for avoiding 'the fatal disconnections of subjects' was not to lose specialist studies within an integrated whole, but rather to teach them for cognitive overspill. The general education he valued was a product of specialist studies taught in a particular kind of way: 'the subjects pursued for the sake of a general education are special subjects specially studied; and, on the other hand, one of the ways of encouraging general mental activity is to foster a special devotion. You may not divide the seamless coat of learning. What education has to impart is an intimate sense for the power of ideas, for the beauty of ideas, and for the structure of ideas, together with a particular body of knowledge which has peculiar reference to the life of the being possessing it.'[24] It is noteworthy that Whitehead's coinage of the metaphor of the seamless coat of learning lies at the centre of his advocacy of the liberal power of *specialized* studies, and this suggests a quite different interpretation from the one usually offered: it is not so much undesirable to divide the seamless coat of learning as impossible, however specialized your teaching. Indeed, in his view, the disposition to seek relationships between ideas is a product of specialist study: 'the appreciation of the structure of ideas is that side of a cultured mind which can only grow under the influence of a special study. I mean that eye for the whole chess-board, for the bearing of one set of ideas on another. Nothing but a special study can give any appreciation for the exact formulation of general ideas, for their relations when formulated, for their service in the comprehension of life'.[25] Whitehead deplored the degeneration of learning into a reception of 'inert ideas'. But, for him, this tendency is not to be avoided by abandoning subject studies so much as by ensuring a concrete reference for abstract principles, and the utilization and testing of ideas by throwing them into ever 'fresh combinations'. Bruner's concept of the spiral curriculum is clearly foreshadowed by Whitehead's prescription, 'let the main ideas which are introduced into a child's education be few and important, and let them be thrown into every combination possible'.[26]

  This quotation from Whitehead does suggest the sense in which all educationists should be concerned with integration. His familiar protest against the accumulation of 'inert ideas' was not a denunciation of education based on the traditional disciplines, though this phrase is often coupled with his image of the seamless coat to justify integration as opposed to subject teaching. Inert knowledge is not that which has no immediate utility for the daily practical concerns of the learner. Knowledge is saved from inertness, as Whitehead implies, by the manner in which it is taught and learned, through the spiral or developmental curriculum in which facts, principles and skills are caught up in a cyclical process of learning; as when, in Whitehead's own terminology, the generalization of one learning cycle becomes the romance of the next. Integrating knowledge and experience does not mean a search for omniscience, so much as taking care that what is being learned now grows out of earlier learning, whether in the same or another discipline, and is related to relevant contexts in other subjects or life outside the classroom.

  Again, to question the educational value of the conception of wholeness as 'an ideal bird's eye view of all knowledge' is not to ignore the importance of developing an integrated, enduring self,[27] by virtue of which our participation in any of life's specialized activities takes on a distinctive character. The tolerant (or fastidious, or rude, or lazy, or intelligent, or industrious) person may display this and other personal characteristics in most of his behaviour. To speak of a person's integrity is, in part, to refer to a certain predictability in his conduct. To use the reproach, 'I would not have expected that of you', is to impugn a person's integrity. Perhaps it is a function of education to build personal integrity in this sense. But so far as this is an acceptable educational aim, it is by no means axiomatic that an exclusively integrated curriculum is the appropriate means of achieving it. We have little or no evidence on this point: indeed it would be difficult to know what sort of evidence would reassure us one way or the other. However, the advantage of taking an agnostic view about the superior claims of any particular kind of curriculum organization to further personal integration is that this transfers our concern to the place where child-centred educationists would want it; that is, away from the notion of an already integrated (and hence artificial) package of human knowledge towards that of an integrating learner. It is interesting that an American study group on the problem of integration should have shifted its point of emphasis in this direction during its deliberations. As its chairman reported: 'We have come to see the problem a little differently. The task is not that of communicating to the individual an integrated view of all knowledge; it is rather that of developing individuals who will seek to do this for themselves ... The integrating person rather than the integrated curriculum became our concern.'[28]

When curricula are integrated by curriculum developers, this raises problems of authority no less than education through the separate disciplines. One of the interesting things about curricula devised in terms of the interests and needs of children is the way in which these often merely reflect adult assumptions about what children *ought* to be interested in, often completely ignoring obvious manifestations of children's interest.[29] It is argued elsewhere that teachers cannot escape responsibility for making these judgments of value on children's behalf (see Chapter 7). But it is important to recognize that the integrated curriculum carries as much danger of authoritarianism and miscalculation about the appropriateness of subject matter as does the curriculum based upon distinctive disciplines.

REFERENCES

1   H. L. CASWELL 'Difficulties in Defining the Structure of the Curriculum' in PASSOW *Curriculum at the Crossroads*, p. 109.

2   SCHOOLS COUNCIL WORKING PAPER No. 11 *Society and the Young School Leaver*, p. 3. H.M.S.O., London, 1967.

3   SIR J. ADAMS *Modern Developments in Educational Practice*, pp. 12–13. University of London Press, 1938.

4   L. CONNELL 'Child-centred or Subject-centred?' *Bulletin of the Institute of Education, University of Leeds*, No. 42, 1963.

5   I. SCHEFFLER *The Language of Education*, Ch. 2.

6   SCHEFFLER, loc. cit.

7   In a report recently circulated by one University Appointments Board (1965) a student was reported as commenting upon his postgraduate teacher training course in another university, 'What I learned at —— is that the child is all important and mathematics is immaterial.'

8   It is interesting, of course, that some child-centred theorists have displayed considerable nostalgia for the uncorrupted, unsophisticated life of the primitive. This point has often been made with reference to Rousseau. It is also implicit in PESTALOZZI's *crie de coeur*: 'Friend! the crimes of Europe are still increasing through idle talk. It is connected with over-civilization, and its results are influencing the conditions of all our feelings, thoughts and actions. It is connected with the far-reaching increase of our Slavery.' *How Gertrude Teaches Her Children*, p. 172; Swann Sonnenschein, London, 1894.

9   T. H. HUXLEY used this concept of artificial education in a commendatory, non-pejorative sense. He also had in mind that artificial education is necessary because Nature is herself a brutal, stern, uncompromising and undiscriminating teacher: 'Nature's discipline is not even a word and a blow, and the blow first; but the blow without the word. It is left to you to find out why your ears were boxed. The object of artificial education is to make good these defects in Nature's methods.' 'How Nature Teaches' in *Collected Essays*, Vol. III, p. 85, Macmillan, London, 1893. However, when DEWEY refers to the 'artificiality of school learning', his usage is in a pejorative sense: see *Democracy and Education*, p. 161. For a fuller discussion of the concept of natural education, see also HARDIE *Truth and Fallacy in Educational Theory*,

Ch. I, and R. J. W. SELLECK *The New Education*, Ch. 6, Pitman, London, 1968.

10 See references to HIRST, HARRÉ and PHENIX, pp. 86–7.

11 A. C. MORETON 'The Creation of an Integrated Course' in *University of Manchester School of Education Gazette*, No. 9, July 1967.

12 M. H. WILSON 'Recipe for Integration' *University of Manchester School of Education Gazette*, No. 8, December 1966.

13 M. L. JACKS *Total Education*. Kegan Paul, Trench & Trubner, 1946.

14 ADVISORY COUNCIL FOR EDUCATION (England and Wales) *Half Our Future* (Newsom Report), Ch. 16. H.M.S.O., London, 1963.

15 See, for example, I. F. ROLLS 'Environmental Studies: a New Synthesis' *Education for Teaching*, Spring 1969. See also SCHOOLS COUNCIL (Welsh Committee) *Environmental Studies*, Schools Council Publications, 1968. Also MORETON AND WILSON, op. cit.

16 MORETON, op. cit.

17 See *The Times Educational Supplement*, 17 January 1969, for an example of the poverty-stricken history which comes out of a project on trees.

18 There is some evidence in a study by B. MYERS *The Map Reading Ability of Some Junior School Children* (University of Manchester Diploma Dissertation, 1969) to support the commonsense assumption that children's understanding of symbols on Ordnance Survey maps develops first in relation to those rural objects (e.g. trees, rivers) where the O.S. symbol bears a closer resemblance to the object symbolized and is less abstract than those from the urban scene (houses and other buildings), or where the object and the symbol stand out more starkly, both on the ground and on the map, in the uncluttered rural landscape (e.g. railway lines, roads).

19 See *The Thirty Third Yearbook of Education*, pp. 59, 110–11, 135; also MINISTRY OF EDUCATION *Primary Education*, p. 59; H.M.S.O., London, 1959.

20 J. DEWEY *The Child and the Curriculum*, p. 22. Phoenix Books, University of Chicago Press, 1959.

21 See W. H. BURSTON *The Principles of History Teaching*,

Methuen, London, 1963. This text discusses the conclusions of different philosophers of history about the nature of historical explanation.

22   R. S. PETERS 'What is an educational process?' in R. S. PETERS (Ed.) *The Concept of Education*. Routledge & Kegan Paul, London, 1967.

23   J. DEWEY, *Democracy and Education*, p. 162.

24   A. N. WHITEHEAD *The Aims of Education*, p. 18. Williams & Norgate, London, 1955.

25   WHITEHEAD, op. cit., pp. 18–19.

26   WHITEHEAD, op. cit., p. 3.

27   L. A. REID *Philosophy and Education*, Ch. 7, Heinemann, London, 1962. See also R. S. PETERS 'Moral Education and the Psychology of Character' *Philosophy*, 1962. Also J. MACMURRAY *The Self as Agent*, Faber & Faber, London, 1957.

28   NATIONAL SOCIETY FOR THE STUDY OF EDUCATION, 'The Integration of Educational Experiences'. *Fifty Seventh Yearbook*, Pt III, pp. 5, 252. University of Chicago Press, 1958.

29   For example, I have noted elsewhere that those who devise curricula in terms of the interests and needs of school leavers, often miss the obvious point that these are interested, above all, in vocational education. See my *Education, Work and Leisure*, op. cit., pp. 80–6.

7: Education for life

The conclusion that separate subjects have a necessary place in the curriculum is sometimes taken to imply acceptance of the educational and cultural *status quo*. Some critics of the subject-orientated approach to education argue that this entails ossification of the curriculum in the form and content it assumed in the nineteenth century. It is assumed that as we sweep towards the twenty-first century we need a curriculum geared to the experience of rapid and radical change which appears to be the condition of humanity in advanced industrial societies. But emphasis upon education for a rapidly changing future is largely irrelevant to the problem of whether the curriculum is subject or project based. Avoiding curricular and cultural stagnation requires constant revaluation of the content of whatever mode of curricular organization we adopt. In particular, we need to be sensitive to novel ways of looking at experience which may be implicit in developments in scientific knowledge, in technological change and social reorganization, or which follow from innovations in the arts and developments in the behavioural disciplines, all implying different possibilities of self-awareness which alter the interests of human beings.

Educationists must always be ready to jettison subject matter and be constantly prepared to find room in the curriculum for new skills and areas of knowledge. But keeping a mind open to the need for change in the curriculum creates the problem of deciding what should be included and what can reasonably be omitted. On what criteria might we exclude Latin or Greek or Euclidian geometry? In accordance with what educational principles do we decide to teach economics, sociology or psychology? How do we approach the claims that metalwork, technical drawing, bookkeeping, chess or sex instruction ought to be in the curriculum? How do we evaluate the suggestion that even Bingo might be justified in schools? (See pp. 133–4 below.) Or, assuming an integrated approach to curriculum construction, are some integrated topics or projects more valuable educationally than others? Does an integrated study focused on the local high street or the local bus route provide insights and disciplines as valuable as studies of the mass-media, problems of race, war and peace and similar issues?

Child-centred educationists have often approached questions of this kind from the assumption that schooling ought to be related to life. It is a familiar theme in contemporary educational literature that for the school leaver, at least, education should have relevance for life 'as he sees it': 'many adolescents are bored and frustrated by their experiences in school, which seem to them to have nothing to do with life as they hope to live it when they grow up'.[1] Criticism of the traditional school often begins from the conclusion that its curriculum stands divorced from life. References to 'real life' as against the life of the school or life as exemplified in the school subjects are common. Indeed, in an effort to dramatize the discrepancy between school and life, it is sometimes suggested that we should look at the curriculum as though we were starting from scratch: if we considered carefully what people really need to know (for example, of mathematics) for the conduct of their daily lives, what a useless load of rubbish the school curriculum would seem.

The slogan 'education for life' has an obvious persuasiveness which it is difficult to resist. Indeed, one prominent nineteenth-century educationist did exploit the emotive implications of life's denial, death. The Danish Latin school where Grundvig[2] and his contemporaries were educated was 'a school for death', an evaluation applying, implicitly, to the entire European grammar school tradition of which the Danish schools were one manifestation. But although the idea is especially attractive that schooling should be linked with life, this immediately raises a number of questions. Ought the school to connect with every conceivable life activity? Are there some things which children have to learn about life that are best learned outside the school, at home or in church, for example? Are not many life activities immoral or culturally barren? In underprivileged communities, will the school fulfil its civilizing function by promoting activities which can have little meaning in the out-of-school experience of the child or for the adults amongst whom he lives? Confronted with this kind of question, advocates of education for life are rarely explicit about the meaning they attach to 'real life'. The danger is that the idea of education for life as the child sees it, or in order to meet 'the problems of day-by-day living of ordinary citizens', will make for shortened perspectives in two directions. First, schooling may become preoccupied with biological, instrumental, hand-to-mouth life activities; secondly, there is a tendency for the *lifelong* dimension of life to be forgotten through a focus upon the ephemeral concerns of youth.

EDUCATIONAL UTILITARIANISM

Some discussions of education for life ignore the fact that life is lived at many different levels and through a multitude of activities varying greatly in content and quality. In particular, proposals for 'life curricula' sometimes prompt the conclusion that their authors believe the only significant part of life to be that segment of it which is lived 'in the market place'. Life is equated with man's daily comings and goings in the streets, in shops, on public transport, at the bank or in the post office and so on. There is a tendency to ignore those life activities which are little concerned with fundamental life requirements for food, clothing and shelter. Much living in the market place is concerned, however covertly, with these biological imperatives of existence and to focus unduly upon this aspect of life is to encourage a preoccupation with the needs and appetites which men share with the brutes. No doubt our ways of satisfying these fundamental animal appetites become increasingly ingenious and sophisticated. Eating and drinking becomes the art of gastronomy; our need for clothing and shelter produce, respectively, *haute couture* and architecture, and it is a legitimate product of education that we learn to satisfy these fundamental appetites with dignity, humanity, taste and style. It cannot be a matter of indifference, intellectually, morally or aesthetically, how we conduct ourselves in the commerce of the market place. But the insistent criticism that Western civilization is 'too materialistic' is usually making the point that a disproportionate measure of human energy and initiative and skill goes into satisfying or sophisticating the 'necessary appetites' at the expense of those activities which nourish the spirit of men. Creative energies are brought into the service of industrial marketing – planning obsolescence and the 'hidden persuasion' of consumer demand, for example – whilst the non-instrumental arts are put at a discount.

Some evidence for the claim that the life curriculum often over-emphasizes these commercial needs can be found by inspection of textbooks of the 'Mathematics (or English) for Citizenship' type. Language or mathematical studies of this kind are apt to focus on the English or arithmetic of the post office, the savings bank, the supermarket or the transport system. Replacing the apparently futile traditional mathematical exercises concerned with problems like that of filling baths without stopping up the plugholes, we have exercises in the calculation of wage rates, income tax, interest on savings, hire purchase, the cost of planting a lawn, papering a room, running a car, or how to estimate from airline timetables the time it would take to fly to Australia. Or language study is reduced to a consideration of those communication situations encountered in filling in forms at the town hall or in cashing National Insurance benefits.

Presumably the justification for this sort of mathematics and language study is that it has a motivational value stemming from its obvious concern with problems located within the 'real life' of the world. In fact, it is questionable whether children see the situation in quite these terms. We do not avoid a school problem being 'academic' merely by choosing it from real life outside school. The 'Arithmetic for Citizenship' type of exercise we have just noted is an academic problem (as common speech has it) if you don't happen to be going to Australia, if you don't own a house or a car and are not in receipt of an income. Whatever the motivational value of this kind of approach to the learning of mathematics, these are not the problems which children encounter spontaneously in the everyday business of life. They are clearly adult problems and are no more real to children than those exercises which are given a spurious concreteness for children by attaching objects to numbers, for example, where children in the early stages of arithmetic are set to add goats to sheep and are asked to give the answer in 'animals'. The fact that children (having done their calculations accurately) have to be reminded to insert the appropriate category (for example, animals) indicates that they are quite willing to do calculations as pure arithmetical puzzles without the need for 'real life' reference. Both types of exercise are academic in the sense that without the school and its apparatus of provided materials the problems would be unlikely to occur to children. Problems which are real for children in the sense of being initiated by them or concerned with some project of importance to them (for example, a Youth Hostel trip) are most likely to occur in connection with extra-curricular activities, and their occasional intra-curricular occurence hardly provides the basis for an adequate mathematics syllabus.

Two further criticisms of this instrumental or utilitarian conception of education are relevant. First, it is sometimes argued that advocacy of a utilitarian curriculum is ultimately against the interests of learners as individuals. An instrumental view of curriculum activities tends ultimately towards the justification of only that subject matter which is socially or economically valued. From the point of view of the State which finances and legislates for education, schooling is seen primarily as an investment, a method of raising industrial production, of solving balance of payments problems or getting ahead in the race to the moon; or it becomes an instrument of the Cold War. In this climate of opinion it is easy to dismiss drama, music, literature, art and recreational activities as educational 'frills'. Natural science, on the other hand, receives considerable support since this can be justified as a sound national investment. Indeed, the language of education sometimes becomes indistinguishable from that of economics: education is an *investment*, schools and colleges are *plants*, graduates are *products* and the salaries of teachers become subject to *productivity agreements*.

Thus criticism of a utilitarian conception of education stems partly from a concern that educationists should not 'sell out' to economists, sociologists, industrialists or the military. The need to maintain a non-instrumental stance in relation to education seems the more necessary since it is assumed that the man in the street (the *consumer* of educational services) is all too ready to value education in economic terms; too sympathetic towards a 'hand-to-mouth' conception of education and insensitive to the contribution which education can make towards the good life. Education seems valued only for the contribution it can make towards life's instrumentalities: how to choose the fastest train, how to open and operate a bank account, how to send a telegram, how to calculate super-tax, how to lay concrete paths and so on.

This points to a second criticism of a curriculum focused upon life in the market place. The positive implications of anti-utilitarianism are that the life curriculum is often inadequate in failing to take cognizance of important life activities which are the distinguishing mark of civilized communities. If education is to be related to life it must focus upon the best conceivable life, the life of 'civilized rational man'. And the point about a great deal of civilized life is that it is a life of play. Many of our characteristically civilized activities have the non-instrumental character of play. This is not merely true of activities like chess, golf, rugger, ludo or Bingo. Pursuits which are highly esteemed in civilized communities – theatre and concert-going, reading poetry, making music and dance, painting and looking at pictures, for example – have the distinguishing features of play. Thus, whilst most of our activity in the market place is instrumental in character, there exists for most men (and increasingly so in highly industrialized communities) a play life whose main characteristic is that it is an area of life in which we can exercise considerable choice of activity. Moreover, much of what we do in this area of life is not vital, since it is a matter of indifference biologically whether we read novels, listen to music, or play Bingo in preference to either of these things. We can refrain from doing all of these things and a great many others without threatening existence itself. Some would think life intolerable without theatre, novels and orchestral concerts, but others manage just as well with bingo or pigeon-fancying.

With the growth of leisure,[3] an increasing proportion of living will be a play life in this sense. But to say that an activity falls within the category of play is not to disparage it. Play is non-serious, non-vital, not in the sense of being trivial or requiring little effort or commitment, but in being a non-instrumental activity, essentially unproductive of economic value.[4] Clearly our play activities have little relevance to the economic problem of 'bringing home the bacon'. But they are serious and important activities in the sense that they constitute much of what civilized living must necessarily be about. It is therefore argued that it is this non-instrumental aspect of life which education should aim to cultivate.

From this point of view, the test of whether an activity should occur in the curriculum is that it is intrinsically valuable, not that it serves some extrinsic end. The proper end of education is 'to help people to discover activities whose ends are not outside themselves . . . The central ability which ought to be the fruit of education serves nothing directly except itself, no one except those who exercise it'. Thus, 'above all the task of education is to teach the value of activity for its own sake'.[5] How acceptable is this criterion that the basis of the curriculum should be those activities which can be pursued primarily for their own intrinsic values?

EDUCATIONAL ACTIVITY FOR ITS OWN SAKE

The conception that educational activities should be engaged in for their own sakes does help to diminish the dangers of educational utilitarianism. As we have just argued, it sanctions those cultural activities which have the non-instrumental character of play and warns against educational preoccupation with only those activities which contribute directly and urgently to national economic well-being. Moreover, it is a necessary correlate of a child-centred emphasis which suspects *preparation* as an educational aim, that many curricular activities must be pursued for their own sakes and not only for whatever contribution they might make to life lived in the distant future. An emphasis upon the educational pursuit of activities having intrinsic interest for the child thus seems essential to the resolution of the present–future antithesis which was discussed in Chapter 5. Again, the pursuit of learning for its own sake should dispose men towards a standpoint in life which is critical, disinterested, rational, impersonal, unaffected by expedience.[6] It helps to safeguard standards of scholarship and truth. It counters the unfortunate tendency to value education primarily as an economic investment with its implication that what is economically valueless may safely be banished from the curriculum. Only its own logic – not the demands of economic or political expedience – should dictate the sort of things men choose to teach and learn. If the resolution of prejudice, the fostering of tolerance and a mature ability to face and act upon unpleasant facts of life are imperative requirements of life in a civilized community, then commitment to learning things for their disciplinary, non-expedient values is important.

The notion of education for its own sake is also the justification for aesthetic education. Where a utilitarian evaluation of education is dominant, those aspects of the curriculum which nourish the aesthetic sensibility – mainly the fine arts – are apt to be the first casualties. The aesthetic standpoint is essentially contemplative, withdrawn from instrumental or practical activity. Hospers argues that the aesthetic attitude 'consists in the separation of aesthetic experience from the needs and desires of everyday life and from the response which we automatically make to our environment as practical human beings . . . the aesthetic attitude can only occur when the practical response to the environment is held in suspension'.[7] Hampshire makes a similar point: the aesthetic standpoint 'is a temporary refusal to classify usefully and to consider the possibilities of action'.[8] It is thus difficult to assimilate aesthetic education within a concept of education as primarily utilitarian or instrumental. From the point of view of the practical contingencies of daily life in the market place – trying to keep body and soul together, raising productivity, balancing the budget, governing states and defending their integrity – aesthetic experience inevitably wears the aspect of something at the fringe of life. It is for the idle, the visionary or the average man when he has nothing better to occupy his leisure time. It is all too easy for parents and teachers to wish aesthetic activities in schools to the periphery of the curriculum when the serious business of learning to live in the market place has been taken care of. The advocacy of activities because they are intrinsically valuable, and not because they minister to some end located outside themselves, is a justification for including things in the curriculum because they are enjoyable and satisfying as and when they happen. In reading poetry, for example, pupils are submitting, there and then, to an aesthetic experience capable of being enjoyable and emotionally satisfying in itself. A poem may contain a moral, it may teach us how to use words or metaphors in novel and interesting ways; or it may offer an opportunity for language study. But as a curriculum activity, a poem may have instrumental value only in the sense that it assists in the development of aesthetic sensibility itself. This possibility of abandon to an educational activity for its sheer aesthetic pleasure is implicit in MacIntyre's claim that in education 'the relation of the mind to what it grasps can be as that of the dancer to the dance'.[9]

However, the insistence upon the pursuit of educational activity for its own sake has dangers. It can be used to justify preoccupation with those esoteric aspects of human knowledge which may interest the specialist or scholar but which have little of the relevance for common experience which would justify their place in a general education. It is recourse to the doctrine of learning for its own sake in order to justify the teaching of obsolete or recondite knowledge which invites the stigma that some educational activities are merely repositories of 'inert ideas'. And when we are in the realm of those activities which are valued for their own sakes, it is very much a matter of one man's meat being another man's poison.

EDUCATIONAL ACTIVITY FOR THE LEARNER'S SAKE

Thus the concept 'for its own sake' is not a sufficient criterion for educational activity and may lead to learning which is barren without the correlate 'for the learner's sake'. Perhaps learning should be disinterested, unaffected by expedience or personal idiosyncrasy. But to be disinterested is not to be uninterested. Moreover, a person cannot know everything that could be known for its own sake. He must choose between a multitude of activities which are intrinsically valuable. And he chooses ultimately on the basis of what interests *him*. Tonight he reads a novel, or listens to music, or goes to a football match for its own sake and not for what it will enable him to do tomorrow. But he chooses also for *his* own sake; because he hopes to enjoy the book or music or game. If he opts for reading or music he must choose one novel or some few records and the choice he makes reflects his moods, his interests, or his being intrigued by a comment he has heard about this symphony or that writer. A person cannot do everything worthwhile that might be done for its own sake, or learn everything that he might find interesting. Choice of activity is always, to that extent, subjective. It reflects individual talent, dispositions, experiences and opportunities, as well as a person's limitations. What we choose to do is chosen from personal interest. In this sense, what is learned matters to the learner. There is 'a reception of convivial information'. Polanyi's concept of 'personal knowing' is relevant here. The acquisition of personal knowledge involves the committed, the interested participation of the learner: 'into every act of knowing there enters a passionate contribution of the person knowing what is being known, and . . . this coefficient is no mere imperfection but a vital component of his knowing'.[10] As Dewey put it, 'Knowledge cannot be the idle view of an unconcerned spectator'.[11] And as well as engaging the interest of the learner, personal knowing confers upon him a sense of power. He knows *how to do* something with what he learns: his learning embraces skills, concepts and principles which he can apply, which he knows how to use in appropriate situations. 'Dead knowledge' or 'inert ideas' are likely to follow from a stress upon learning for its own sake when this is divorced from a concept of the learner as one having interests, concerns, purposes, talents, dispositions and a point of view which is entirely his own.

9

However, by itself, the notion of education for the learner's sake is also an insufficient basis upon which to build the curriculum. As we noted at the beginning of this chapter, there is an insistent persuasion towards the provision of educational activities which are related to life 'as the child sees it'. This is particularly true of a great deal of post-Newsom curriculum development. It is difficult to escape the conclusion that following the advice to relate the curriculum to the life of the school leaver 'as he sees it', would often involve the school in abdicating its function to raise the level of individual and public intelligence and taste. Life as the child sees it is often sordid, culturally barren, without hope. For this reason alone, the child's own horizons often impose quite unacceptable limitations upon the curriculum. It is a dangerous prescription that the school should affiliate with life if this means building the curriculum upon the standards of the culturally underprivileged. We ought to expect that the school will attempt to raise the cultural standards of the community, that it will affiliate with the best life outside the school. We must view with circumspection the idea that because out-of-school life is 'real life', it is, therefore, the school which should adjust to the out-of-school interests of the child. Jersild's examination of children's interests indicated that 'the range of children's out-of-school interests is quite restricted compared with children's potentialities'.[12] In terms of the child's capacity to acquire interests it may be that the school's concern to educate the child away from its real-life interests is the most realistic course to take. The problem for a 'related to life' view of the school is: which competing life values ought the school to mediate? And there is a danger that the pursuit of life relevance and interest through the neighbourhood type of environmental study aiming at social adjustment, will become an educational device not essentially different in its social implications from the nineteenth-century conception of popular education as something designed to confirm the learner in his divinely ordered, but modest, station in life.[13]

But however culturally deprived his environment, and however limited his aspirations, the temptation to forge links with life as the child sees it is strong. A severe problem of motivation follows from the fact that children may reject what the school offers as irrelevant to their cultural opportunities in a home or neighbourhood which, for any educated person, may have severe limitations (see Chapter 11). But even to think of motivation as a problem implies that the teacher cannot rest content with the cultural standards which are accepted by the learner, or be satisfied with the sort of learning which the child is prepared to undertake spontaneously. To see motivation as a problem is to recognize that, initially, the content of the curriculum will not have an intrinsic appeal for its own sake and that the teacher has an inspirational function to perform. He is confronted with the task of bringing the young to 'the peak in Darien',[14] of revealing cultural realms beyond their own imaginings. To ensure that education develops 'out of the needs and interests of children' necessitates our being sensitive to what *they* find pleasurable, amusing, challenging. But it also involves us in calculating how to bridge the gap between the world of here and now and the deeper, wider, human experience which the teacher, enjoying and finding valuable, must want to communicate. The teacher's responsibility is to affirm his belief in the importance of activities which are culturally valuable.

EDUCATION AND CULTURALLY VALUABLE ACTIVITIES

It is apparent that the concepts of 'activity for its own sake' and 'for the learner's sake' are necessary but insufficient criteria for curriculum building. As well as justifying obsolete knowledge having no power to quicken the imagination of the learner, they can, together, be used to justify activities which are undemanding, trivial, even immoral. They must be applied subject to the condition that an activity is not mis-educational or otherwise unethical. Cruelty, for example, is not always practised instrumentally: sadistic, apparently motiveless crime is, presumably, intrinsically satisfying to the criminal. It is an activity engaged in for its own sake, much the same as other people read books, go to the theatre, listen to music or play rugger. Hence the importance of this third necessary criterion: the curriculum must consist of activities which are culturally valuable.

Broadly, 'culture' has come to acquire two distinctive meanings. Historically, the word has a normative, evaluative reference; but alongside this there has developed a value-free, descriptive usage. The former is to be found mainly in a tradition of literary and social criticism and its best known delineation is in Matthew Arnold's *Culture and Anarchy*. As Arnold conceived it, culture is 'the pursuit of perfection'. This 'perfection . . . is a harmonious expansion of *all* the powers which make the beauty and worth of human nature'. And, especially, this pursuit of 'our total perfection' is a process 'of getting to know, on all the matters which most concern us, the best which has been thought and said in the world'.[15] This *best* of human thought has often been sought in the arts (especially literature) and philosophy, a fact which sometimes attracts the appellation 'Third Programme Culture'.

Against this stands the anthropological, descriptive sense of culture as 'a whole way of life'. In this sense, not merely does a culture include activities which are approved (as in the normative sense) but also, presumably, activities which are commonly regarded as immoral or criminal, as well as those which evoke no such evaluations. This concept of culture has been epitomized in the now familiar words of T. S. Eliot: 'It includes all the characteristic activities and interests of a people: Derby Day, Henley Regatta, Cowes, the twelfth of August, a cup final, the dog races, the pin table, the dart board, Wensleydale cheese, boiled cabbage cut into sections, beetroot in vinegar, nineteenth-century Gothic churches and the music of Elgar'.[16] Eliot invites the reader to make his own list.

It is difficult to envisage how education – itself a normative concept[17] – can pursue cultural objectives except in the evaluative sense just outlined. The disciplinary functions of the school require that it discriminates amongst the manifold activities which aggregate the total pattern of life in a community. In the sociological sense of culture, some strands in the cultural pattern are technologically or economically disfunctional, some aggravate social injustice, others offend the moral and aesthetic sensibilities and many make for the impoverishment of the intellect and the emotions. Thus, the educationist has no escape from the conclusion that, in schools, opportunity should be provided for engagement only with those activities which have disciplinary values in promoting growth of intellectual capacity and aesthetic and moral sensibility.

It is for this reason that a cultural activity like Bingo, which has recently been defended as a worthwhile educational activity,[18] can have no place in the curriculum of the school. Bingo is an activity having no disciplinary value whatever. Only in a very minimal sense does it have to be learned at all. Anyone who is able to recognize numbers up to one hundred can play Bingo. The parent discovering that his child had been 'learning' to play Bingo in school would rightly protest at the waste of time in 'teaching' an activity which he himself could 'teach' his child in five minutes. For not only are the rules and principles of the game comprehensively explained in a few minutes: unlike many so-called games of chance (card games, for example) Bingo is a purely chance affair, admitting of no initiative whatever from the player; all that he needs to do is keep awake and prevent his attention from wandering. Bingo is a game without a strategy or tactics. It makes no sense to talk about mastery of the game since the player is permitted no freedom or initiative to manœuvre within the rules. And if no two games of Bingo are exactly alike, in the sense that there is considerable possible permutation of the order in which the numbers are called, this variety is in no way a consequence of the way in which the players deploy their skill. To say that someone is good at Bingo is merely to say that he is lucky, not that he is skilful. There is no skill involved in playing Bingo and it is difficult to understand how anyone who really knew the game could affirm, 'I am fairly sure that some do, and quite certain that one could . . . benefit educationally from Bingo'[19]: or that something like Bingo 'can be done "seriously" and results, then, in the development of "conceptual schemes and forms of appraisal which transform everything else" '.[20]

However, the defence of Bingo has a larger purpose in the educational debate than the mere assertion of the cultural values of this particular game. Bingo is a symbol for all those activities which define the sub-culture of the working class. For reasons we have suggested, it happens to be a poor exemplar of the point at issue, namely, that many so-called working class activities have moral, aesthetic and intellectual dimensions which at least equal the conventional content of what has traditionally been thought to characterize the 'best' culture. However inappropriately, the defence of Bingo epitomizes a widespread dissatisfaction with a traditional curriculum which appears to have developed exclusively in terms of those activities which characterize the culture of the middle classes. English secondary education (particularly the grammar school) is often criticized for its preoccupation with middle class values and its ignoring of other cultural traditions. The assumption that schooling has traditionally been concerned with the transmission of middle class culture is one of the unexamined assumptions in English educational theory. However, criticism of this view would take us far outside the scope of this chapter. The question really being raised in the debate about Bingo is whether there are not other activities which have cultural values but which have not hitherto commended themselves to those who legislate for school curricula.

It is at this point that the anthropological conception of total cultural configuration becomes pertinent to the discussion of the curriculum. Our culture has to be examined for hitherto neglected activities which measure up to the disciplinary requirements of the curriculum. Have schools in the past been too often concerned with a literary culture as the only important source of valuable life interests and insights and too little committed to helping children to explore the educational values of other forms of cultural activity? Have the other arts, especially the practical arts, found their due place? Has the literary culture itself been unduly classical in conception? Have the meanings and educational implications of a scientific culture been properly explored? As Raymond Williams[21] shows, the debate about culture over two centuries has been conducted largely by literary figures and it is, perhaps, understandable that their notions of 'the best culture' have been exemplified in terms of that particular cultural manifestation with which they were most familiar. Williams indicates the dangers of an undue preoccupation with literary culture: 'There is an evident danger of delusion, to the highly literate person, if he supposes that he can judge the quality of general living by primary reference to the reading artifacts . . . Many highly educated people have, in fact, been so driven on in their reading, as a stabilizing habit, that they fail to notice that there are other forms of skilled, intelligent creative activity: not only the cognate forms of theatre, concert, and picture-gallery; but the whole range of general skills, from gardening, metalwork, and carpentry to active politics. The contempt for many of these activities, which is always latent in the highly literate, is a mark of the observers' limits, not those of the activities themselves. Neglect of the extraordinary popularity of many of these activities, as evidence of the quality of living in contemporary society', is the result of partisan selection'.[22] Arnold might certainly be faulted for wanting to judge the quality of a person's experience from his reading habits: 'a man's life each day depends for its solidity and value on whether he reads during that day, and, far more still, on what he reads during it.'[23] But the essence of Arnold's concept of culture was its normative reference (his concern with improvement)[24] and this remains pertinent to any discussion of the cultural functions of the school. The primarily literary orientation of Arnold's thought is of far less importance than his insistence upon the qualitative element in culture. To meet the charge that Arnoldian culture is an essentially middle class conception, having little relevance for the education of the working class, it is merely necessary to assimilate his notion of the *best* with Eliot's idea of culture as a broad range of human activities of many levels and types. As well as to literature, music and art, the notion of perfection can apply to association football, pigeon fancying, do-it-yourself, Lancashire hotpot, Yorkshire pudding, jam on bread – to instance activities and preoccupations which are recognizable components of the culture of the working class. Sport, food and drink are activities which admit discrimination, taste and improvement, no less than the fine arts ('culture does not set itself against the games and sports').[25] To see the educational problem in class terms, and to assert the value of working class cultural activities, does not require the abandonment of the normative for the anthropological concept of culture: Arnold simply requires interpretation through Eliot.

With reference to education it is also necessary to spiralize or 'Brunerize' the concept of culture. Whatever range of activities we judge to be valuable for the culture of the person, these must be seen as existing at different levels of sophistication and embodying key principles and skills capable of development. For example, critics have analysed the music of Lennon and McCartney for its echoes of Bach. Others have found this comparison pretentious, even spurious. Nevertheless, the Beatles promise to be a more enduring musical and literary phenomenon than most manifestations of the 'pop' music scene: it is by no means fanciful to credit them with artistic development. One suspects they may have left some of their earlier admirers behind and those who have developed with them have subtler musical tastes than they began with. But their ultimate aesthetic merit is irrelevant to this fact that their (and some others') popular music contains the key musical elements of rhythm, harmony and melody. The point is that the adolescent with his 'pop' music has a musical culture capable of sustaining critical and disciplined evaluation and even (for those who cannot envisage the possibility of a catholic musical taste which savours both the Beatles and Bach) a growth point for better things to come. In this connexion one recalls a comment of the 'cellist Tortelier after playing Bach: 'See, it is the jazz'.

This emphasis upon meeting the learner where he is serves to emphasize that as with the notion of educational activity for its own sake and for the learner's sake, the idea of culturally valuable activities cannot be the sole criterion for evaluating the claims of a curriculum related to life. Culturally valuable educational activity must complement the notions of educational activity for its own and the learner's sake. Without these correlates, the idea that we have a responsibility to initiate the young into culturally valuable activities carries overtones of paternalism, the authoritarian dangers of which are diminished by a willingness to meet the learner where he is and by attempting to discover amongst his interests and tastes, activities which are capable of disciplined development.

EDUCATION FOR LIFELONG LIFE

However, children's interests and preoccupations are only valuable as curricular activities so long as they are capable of supporting disciplined growth. We have already suggested that the life activities of children and the materials of their immediate environment are valuable educational data mainly as concrete exemplification of the concepts and principles which provide life insights beyond the situations in which they are learned. Exclusive focus upon the immediate life situations of the learner may be a disservice to him. The popular assumption has to be resisted that we best prepare young people for life simply through a head-on confrontation with the problems and dilemmas of contemporary life; by teaching the young to face the problems they will encounter on leaving school through a direct and exclusive focus on those problems. In a valid sense in which education is a preparation for life, it must be preparation for 'lifelong life', not merely for an adolescence lived at a particular place and point in time. Education for life should include the life of the pensioner: indeed, a person's ability to cope with the problems of retirement may depend upon the quality of his formal education when young. Hence a school leaver is educated for life, not merely so far as he carries away from school a description of current social problems and their proposed solutions, but rather to the extent that he is conversant with principles which will assist in an understanding of social and personal problems throughout life. Particularly in the twentieth century, the young are ill served by advocacy of educational activity which is instrumental towards solving present day problems; problems which may not exist (or which will manifest themselves in a radically different form) by the end of the century when today's school leavers will still only be in middle age. Our obsession with youth should not obscure the fact that it is the middle-aged who run our affairs, especially in politics. It is an illusion that we can somehow educate youth to avoid making the mistakes which we have made. As anyone in middle age knows, the social problems facing contemporary Britain are not those which characterized their youth during the first half of the twentieth century. Then, 'strong drink' rather than drug addiction seemed the pitfall confronting the growing adolescent; cyclical rather than technological unemployment (with their quite different implications for geographical mobility) was the major economic dilemma. The moral and social problems of race were virtually unknown in Britain itself. But, paradoxically, the successful outcome of the campaign to solve problems of colonialism through liquidation of the British Empire is a source both of our racial tensions in contemporary Britain and of the spirit of nationalism which threatens to tear Africa and Asia apart, whilst nationalism (the obsession of the inter-war years) declines in Europe.

Consequently the people best fitted to adjust to the problems of contemporary Britain are not those who were taught in their youth to put their faith in the temperance movement, the League of Nations, the Soviet Union, the British Commonwealth (or whatever other panacea for social amelioration), but those whose understanding of their environment was rooted in more fundamental ideas. A general understanding of the principles of ethics, which apply alike to the problems of drug addiction, drink, race, poverty and aggressive nationalism is preferable in education to a description of the solution which a particular generation finds for its own local problems. We prepare for life in both its contemporary and longer term perspectives by encouraging a disciplined consideration of moral principles, using whatever personal and social problems currently confront the young as concrete data to *exemplify* the perennial problems of personal discipline and social conscience which confront human beings, largely irrespective of time and place. If education ought really to be directed towards assisting the learner to cope with the daily contingencies of life throughout his lifetime (including those problems he confronts as an adolescent school leaver), it ought to make him familiar with fundamental modes of thought in relation to wide areas of human experience. Indeed, insistence upon the study of disciplines is an important safeguard against the danger that learning becomes obsolete in periods of rapid change.

The problem is not therefore one of choosing between

academic subjects or a life curriculum, so much as teaching the academic disciplines through concrete exemplar situations drawn from life, whether from contemporary life, life in the past, or life as it may be imagined in the future. The traditional curriculum (assumed to be concerned with a dead past) is sometimes contrasted with the life curriculum devised to help us in the present to shape our future. But to focus upon present dilemmas can be as much a threat to the future as concern for the past is often assumed to threaten the present. It is a valid criticism of some curricular projects which are conceived in terms of finding solutions to social problems, that they intimate little of what might constitute the good life if our social dilemmas were resolved. It is irrelevant to this criticism that, on a global basis, our social problems are unlikely to be solved this side of Utopia. The vision which moves men must have, as well as a passion for social amelioration, some conception of the good life which characterizes an ideal existence. It is true that much educational theory is too Utopian to be a satisfactory working tool for practical educationists (see Chapter 11). But we cannot afford to be so 'down to earth' that we never contemplate life's possibilities if only things were different. In fact, Utopia, like the Kingdom of God, is within men. Its values are essentially those we discover in our best selves and in the dignity, altruism, integrity and capacity for enjoyment of other people. Schooling which is relevant to life cannot avoid this concern with activities and modes of thought and experience which ought to characterize the good life in any community. This is why the normative concept of culture remains an important educational instrument, even when our concern is with the whole way of life of a community.

REFERENCES

1 'Life is too fast for schools', *The Guardian*, 25 September 1965.
2 See P. MANNICHE *Living Democracy in Denmark*, G. E. C. Gad, Copenhagen, 1952.
3 For reservations about the likely extent of available leisure

in an automated society, see my *Education, Work and Leisure,* op. cit.

4   J. HUIZINGA *Homo Ludens,* Ch. I. Routledge & Kegan Paul, London, 1949.

5   A. C. MACINTYRE 'Against Utilitarianism' in HOLLINS (Ed.) *Aims in Education,* p. 9.

6   Ibid.

7   J. HOSPERS *Meaning and Truth in the Arts,* p. 14. University of North Carolina Press, 1946.

8   S. HAMPSHIRE *Thought and Action,* pp. 244–5. Chatto & Windus, London, 1959.

9   MACINTYRE, op. cit.

10 M. POLYANI *Personal Knowledge,* p. viii. Routledge & Kegan Paul, London, 1958.

11 J. DEWEY *Democracy and Education,* p. 338.

12 JERSILD and others *Children's Interests.* Teacher's College Publications, Columbia University, New York, 1949.

13 For an excellent critique of the cultural implications of local environmental studies, see J. WHITE 'Instruction in Obedience', *New Society,* 2 May 1968.

14 Keats's sonnet 'On First Looking into Chapman's Homer' is an excellent corrective to the view of the adolescent as a 'crazy mixed-up kid'; it is itself an adolescent's comment on the liberating effect of book learning.

15 M. ARNOLD *Culture and Anarchy,* pp. 6, 11. Cambridge University Press, 1960.

16 T. S. ELIOT *Notes Towards a Definition of Culture,* p. 31. Faber & Faber, London, 1948.

17 See R. S. PETERS 'What is an educational process?' in PETERS (Ed.) *The Concept of Education.*

18 P. S. WILSON 'In Defence of Bingo', *British Journal of Educational Studies,* Vol. XV, No. 1.

19 Ibid., p. 16.

20 Ibid., p. 11. However, to argue that Bingo lacks the necessary disciplinary merit to justify its inclusion in the school curriculum is not to maintain that it is not a game worth playing outside school itself. Daily life is lived at so many different levels and people often simply need to relax with an activity which makes little demand upon their personal resources. Moreover, precisely because of its failure to demand all but the minimum of knowledge

from the player, Bingo is an ideal family game. The family confined by the weather to its holiday cottage in the country might find it a worthwhile activity in that context, arousing a certain excitement in young and old alike and promoting sociability. The current debate in educational literature about worthwhile activities often ignores this distinction between what is worth doing in an extra-curricular life situation and what has those worthwhile disciplinary values to justify the expenditure upon it of scarce human and material resources in the school. Many enjoyable life activities require only the minimal learning which is usually adequately catered for by daily life itself. The economics of education are such that scarce resources ought not to be employed in practising activities which are easily learned from life or in other educational institutions like the home. Of course, none of this is to argue that a teacher of number in a primary school might not legitimately play Bingo with a class in order to motivate the learning or bring interest to the testing of number recognition. She might even invent an arithmetical bingo designed to practise speed in mental and arithmetical calculation (e.g. calling $25 - 9 + 17$, instead of 33). But Bingo is then merely an instrumental activity, justified on the grounds of facilitating learning of difficult mathematical skills. In this event, the activity which is educationally justifiable is mathematics, and appropriate teaching devices (like Bingo) must be assessed for their technical value in furthering this particular disciplinary activity.

21 R. WILLIAMS *Culture and Society* 1780–1950. Penguin Books, 1961.

22 Ibid., pp. 297–8.

23 ARNOLD, op. cit., p. 6.

24 ARNOLD, op. cit., p. 46.

25 ARNOLD, op. cit., p. 61.

8: The child as agent of his own education

Some educationists find the very notion of teaching anathema, seeming afraid lest they be identified as teachers. An influential contemporary example of this is Carl Rogers, a client-centred, psychotherapist who has attempted to draw educational inferences from his professional experiences. He believes that 'the outcomes of teaching are either unimportant or hurtful'.[1] Froebel apparently held a similar belief that the teacher constitutes a threat to the child: 'education in instruction and- training, originally and in its first principles, should necessarily be *passive*, following (only guarding and protecting), not *prescriptive, categorical*, interfering'. He concluded that 'a more arbitrary (active), prescriptive and categorical interfering education . . . must of necessity annihilate, hinder and destroy'.[2] Whilst avoiding the polemical overtones of these strictures upon teaching, Piaget, in one of his few direct references to schooling, implies that deliberate intentional teaching may be less fruitful than spontaneous concept formation by the child: 'I do not believe that new concepts even at school level are always acquired through adult didactic intervention. This may occur but there is a much more productive form of instruction: the so called "activity schools" endeavour to create situations that, whilst not spontaneous in themselves, evoke spontaneous elaboration on the part of the child, if one manages both to spark his interests and to present the problem in such a way that it corresponds to the structures he has already formed for himself'.[3] Implicit in each of these quotations is the requirement that the teacher must be prepared to yield up the initiative in the educational encounter, assuming a much less active role than the child. Pupil self-activity is the key to learning: the child becomes the agent of his own education.

No doubt there is an element of moral condemnation in some of these denunciations of the activity of teaching. In using words like damaging, hurtful, annihilate, hinder and destroy, these writers locate themselves amongst those whose educational philosophy is anti-authoritarian. In part, they are questioning the moral right of teachers to pose as arbiters of the truth about the universe or as mediators of a culture which may seem alien to the child. We have already discussed the belief that authority must degenerate into authoritarianism and that the teacher, as an authority and a disciplinarian, constitutes a threat to the child's integrity and his freedom (see Chapter 4). But, as was also noted above, the Piagetian-inspired insistence upon post-poning much of the formal learning which occurs in schools derives its justification from psychological rather than moral insights (see Chapter 5). And the passage just quoted from Piaget is notably free of the emotively and morally charged terminology of Froebel and Rogers. This underlines the point that the concept of the active child as against the passive teacher requires discussion of technical as well as moral educational concepts (see Chapter 1, pp. 17–18). Having settled to one's satisfaction the question of the *right* of anyone to teach anyone else, there are distinctively psychological concepts which require elaboration: 'What does it mean to claim that the child can only learn through his own self activity?' 'What exactly is being argued in the assertion that it is impossible to teach anything to anyone else?' 'Is there any sense in which someone might be said to have taught another person?'.

CHILD-CENTRED EDUCATION AS ANTI-DIDACTIC

The stress upon child-initiated learning is undoubtedly a protest against the predominantly didactic teaching methods tradition-ally employed in schools. Historically, schools were mainly teacher-centred in the sense that the phrase 'chalk and talk, accurately epitomized teaching method. Comenius, sometimes called the father of modern educational method, claimed to have found in class teaching a pedagogical device as important as the printing press. In principle, classes could expand indefinitely, the only limitation on numbers being imposed by the size of the available room (a principle capitalized under the monitorial system). This economically motivated practice of multiplying the number of children taught by one teacher was bound to have, as one of its consequences, a concentration on teaching as mainly an activity of *telling*. Inevitably, the most active person in the classroom was the teacher, the child's contribution being confined to monosyllabic answers in response to the teacher's questions.

Under this régime of mass class teaching, children – at least some children – did learn something. Those who understood the talk and felt inclined to learn did profit from the experience. But some, from limited intellectual capacity, and others (not always the dull) from boredom or lack of inclination, failed to learn. This limitation of uni-directional talk or telling in the classroom is underlined by the distinction which Scheffler has drawn between the 'success' and the 'intention' use of the verb 'to teach'. To be teaching with the intention of achieving some goal does not, in itself, ensure the success of the enterprise: 'If Jones is engaged in teaching, he is, then, trying. It is clear that to be trying to do something is not always to succeed. Whether success is obtained depends upon factors outside one's trying: the universe must co-operate'.[4] And part of the co-operating universe is the child.

Though perhaps obvious, the implications of this distinction between 'success' and 'intention' in teaching are not always evident in the classroom. Student teachers are sometimes criticized by examiners because they seem keener to teach than to promote children's learning. The point of such criticism is that they often seem so concerned to display their own virtuoso command of teaching techniques (narration, use of audio-visual materials etc.) that they fail to observe the effect upon children of their own histrionics, or to promote the kind of activity which is as essential to children's mastery as are their own efforts to clarify material. They succeed in telling, but not always in teaching. And the fault of mistaking telling for teaching is not merely one of inexperience. It is an occupational hazard of the experienced teacher. We are always apt to be laying down the law without discovering how far our pupils understand it and can recognize the situations in which it applies. Or, through our penchant for declamation, we resort to driving rather than leading, an activity likely to provoke resistance from the driven. Nevertheless, as Scheffler shows, it is possible to teach even factual information without telling this to the pupil. We can arrange for him to infer it from other statements or to read it up for himself. And putting the child in a position to reason things out for himself from provided information which implies other facts is a familiar way of teaching him.

LEARNING AS A PROBLEM-SOLVING ACTIVITY

This notion that the teacher may best promote learning when he deliberately leaves materials in the path of children derives its rationale from the assumption that learning most readily occurs when the child is located in a problem-solving situation. This conception was popularized by Dewey who stressed the heuristic value of 'the forked-path situation': learning is most likely to follow when a person finds himself in the sort of dilemma represented, metaphorically, as a parting of the ways.[5]

However, Dewey's conception of the problem-initiated learning situation differed somewhat from Piaget's. A considerable degree of teacher initiative is implied in Piaget's reference (see p. 142) to adults creating situations, presenting problems, sparking the child's interests. But Dewey insisted upon the superior educational value of problems encountered by the learner in the conduct of his own affairs rather than those of the teacher's contriving:

'The giving of problems, the putting of questions, the assigning of tasks, the magnifying of difficulties, is a large part of school work. But it is indispensable to discriminate between genuine or simulated or mock problems. The following questions may aid in making such discriminations. (*a*) Is there anything but a problem? Does the question naturally suggest itself within some situation or personal experience? Or is it an aloof thing, a problem only for the purposes of conveying instruction in some school topic? Is it the sort of trying that would arouse observation and engage experimentation outside of school? (*b*) Is it the pupil's own problem, or is it the teacher's or textbook's problem, made a problem for the pupil only because he cannot get the required mark or be promoted or win the teacher's approval, unless he deals with it? Obviously, these two questions overlap. They are two ways of getting at the same point: Is the experience a personal thing of such a nature as inherently to stimulate and direct observation of the connections involved, and to lead to inference and its testing? Or is it imposed from without, and is the pupil's problem simply to meet the external requirement?[6]

It is interesting that although Dewey offered these questions as a heuristic device (to aid discrimination) they were, for him, purely rhetorical and in no sense open questions. The child-initiated problem or project situation was, for Dewey, the paradigm of the self-activated learning situation. Nevertheless, in this discussion they may be taken as genuine questions. How far can education be left, in this way, to the contingencies of the learner's own felt needs?

It is evident that spontaneously encountered problems are often a stimulus towards learning in adults. We usually begin to learn gardening, not by enrolling in an evening class for a systematic course in horticulture, but by attempting to solve particular, limited, immediate problems in piecemeal fashion: how to plant or prune roses, how to lay a lawn and so on. A problem of this sort usually prompts us to consult neighbours or colleagues, or to buy or borrow a book on the subject. But even this is likely to be used as a work of reference: it is unlikely that one would read through a gardening manual as a course of study or work out 'exercises' in the garden just for practice. One is more likely to consult merely the chapter on roses, or look up the index for the pages on planting or pruning, according to the task immediately in hand. Clearly, adult learning often begins with urgent practical problems and proceeds piecemeal as the situation develops. But often this is not the end of the story. Learning need not stop when answers have been found to specific urgent practical problems. A limited encounter with gardening may whet one's appetite for more. Work in the garden may become interesting in itself, stimulating or relaxing, offering challenges worth mastering, a source of recreation rather than a merely utilitarian pursuit. So there comes a point where one might enrol in a systematic course of study in an evening class. But enrolment in evening classes may not even have such an initial practical impetus. The little one knows of a writer or composer, or of philosophy or politics, as a result of unsystematic reading or listening or being on the edge of what appears to be a well-informed discussion by one's colleagues, may be the stimulus to engaging in a planned and disciplined course of study which is either of no immediate practical value or whose 'pay off' may be only in the long run. And it is worth noting that although these adult problems are undoubtedly 'real', they are not always spontaneously encountered. Some of the problems we set ourselves to solve as adults are suggested by other people: 'Have you ever thought of . . .' or 'You would find x interesting'.

How far does this example of the way in which adults learn throw light upon the relative values of child-initiated learning as against courses of study set by teachers? Many practising teachers would think that the circumstances in which adults continue their education have little relevance to the work of the schools. The adult chooses whether, how and when he will learn. And although the growth of adult classes indicates that many adults do feel compelled to continue their education in formal situations, a majority feels no such imperative need for systematic study. Against this, from the child's point of view, schools are created by adults, attendance is compulsory and all the things which follow from the institutionalization of learning must occur irrespective of his own inclinations. However, one thing which clearly does emerge from our description of the usual direction of adult learning, from the spontaneously encountered problem to the disciplined course of study, is that in schools we often get our priorities wrong. In schools, the systematically organized coverage of material – in Whitehead's terminology (see Appendix), the *precision* stage of learning – is often the beginning as well as the end of the learning situation. Indeed, much learning in schools consists of nothing but precision. Yet, on the adult model, the realization of a need for or development of an interest in disciplined systematic learning arises from a piecemeal, often fortuitous encounter with subject matter whilst attempting to solve a problem; either an urgent practical problem like pruning roses or an intellectual puzzlement about an author or composer or philosopher. Since problems of this kind serve as a stage of *romance*, often prompting the adult to adventure towards the disciplined mastery of a subject or skill, so it would seem that children's motivation towards learning might be quickened if courses of study could be developed out of the sort of problems they encounter in 'real life'.

We have already discussed how far the subjects of the curriculum may draw their illustrative data from children's life experiences and how, viewed developmentally, the academic disciplines may be structured in order to explain the developing experiences of the child (see Chapter 5). But to argue that the learner's life problems, concerns and interests may function as the raw materials of disciplined and systematic study is not to assume that the child himself is always able to see the pedagogical implications of his daily encounters with life. That the child cannot see the educational potential of his own experience is essentially the standpoint of those educationists who have questioned the desirability of the child-initiated curriculum. Critics of Dewey have argued that problem-solving is a pedagogical device appropriate only to the mature learner since the ability to recognize the existence of problems is a product of experience and background knowledge: 'All through his exposition Dewey seems too much to assume that the ability to recognize the presence of problems is a matter of little or no difficulty . . . What Dewey fails to make sufficiently clear is the enormous dependence of even the modern scientist on past knowledge before the presence of a problem can be recognized and an hypothesis formulated'.[7] Peters has made a similar point with reference to history in schools. He refers critically to the practice of using historical materials 'to provide riders for problem-solving' believing 'that one has to be, to a certain extent, a historian in order to understand a historical problem'.[8] Jersild[9] has produced evidence to support this view. He concluded that children are often unable to identify the existence of problems which touch them closely. He noted that the deprived child tended not to ask for things which might mitigate his deprivation, except that the chronically hungry child showed an interest in food. Children deprived in other senses (for example, the child living in a slum) were unaware of their deprivation. 'The deprived child' is an adult concept and the child himself cannot always know that it is in his best interests that the circumstances of his deprivation should be removed. And even where Jersild's children were aware of fears, they rarely expressed a wish for help or understanding in overcoming these, or showed any recognition that schooling might help them to come to grips with themselves or their problems. As well as being unaware of things which they might enjoy knowing, they do not appreciate what dangers they are in. And this applies no less to the possible mischievous effects of things like the mass media than to the ill consequences of physical privation. We organize a child's learning partly to avoid his being let down by his experiences. Putting it this way underlines Jersild's point 'that it is necessary to go beyond the study of children's expressed interests in order to get clues to what the educational program should include'.

However, only on the extreme view that a teacher's intervention must be harmful to the child does the point about the inhibiting effect of children's ignorance constitute a conclusive argument against the use of problem-solving as a pedagogical instrument. Problems which might be posed in the classroom lie on a spectrum, one extreme of which is the child's spontaneously encountered dilemma, the other being the rhetorical question of the teacher implying, 'Sit quietly and listen and I'll tell you'. Between these limits there lies a considerable range of possibilities in which teachers help to formulate problems with more or less assistance from children. For example, we can imagine situations in which teachers pose questions to focus attention upon pertinent materials or in order to stimulate children's own research activities. Whether a teacher's questions issue in genuine problem-solving situations or whether they are used merely as a justification for *providing* a list of points (for example, the causes of a war) which children merely learn to parrot is largely a matter of how far children have been genuinely involved in a dialogue throughout the lesson. There is some evidence that children have no wish to take over the initiative in providing study topics. They do not resent their teachers posing problems from unfamiliar areas of knowledge. They merely want an opportunity to talk about subject matter which they find teachers narrating in the spirit of 'Take it or leave it – just remember it and don't ask awkward questions'. Their ideal may merely be to become involved in a conversation about the meaning of presented materials. The child in the classroom where the typical routine is a narrative followed only by dictated notes may long to be placed in a problem-solving situation. But dissatisfaction with the other extreme is expressed by the child who wrote: 'The school I'd like . . . would *not* have about six projects a term – only about one. The reason for this is that I get tired of having to bring newspaper cuttings, matchboxes etc., to school every day, and knowing that by the time we have finished one project, there's always another looming up'.[10] This recalls a judgement once made on Dewey's problem-solving theory of learning: that it merely gave philosophical respectability to the commonsense complaint that 'Life's just one damned thing after another'. Nevertheless, it is possible to capitalize upon the stimulus to learning provided by problems without conveying the impression that life is just a perpetual treadmill. And in deciding who should pose the problems it is as well to remember that some of our more fruitful learning experiences throughout life occur in responding to the stimulus of other people's questions. The problems we strive to solve are not merely those over which we stumble spontaneously, but also those which others leave in our path, often quite deliberately. And the compulsion upon children to attend school is justified largely on the assumption that the young ought to be confronted with dilemmas which would not occur to them if left to their own devices.

LEARNING BY DOING

Whatever one's view about the desirability or possibility of building the curriculum upon a basis of the child's own problems, the emphasis which is often placed upon problem-solving is justified in terms of the psychology of learning. The educational importance of problem-solving derives, in part, from the recognition that ultimately one can only learn to do anything by doing it. Whatever the skill to be learned – preaching, teaching, advocacy at law, scientific research, writing history, diagnosing disease, reading or arithmetical calculation, as well as sawing wood, soldering metal, baking Yorkshire pudding – it can only ultimately be learned by practising it and in no other way. For example, the student teacher who has merely been lectured on the use of the cine-projector will probably find himself utterly baffled on first trying to thread a film into a projector: he would be well advised to practise well in advance if he plans to set up a film lesson in the few minutes available between periods. At all educational levels there is a tendency to want to teach skills by reference to theory alone and the slogan, 'we learn *to do* by doing', stresses an important principle which has too often been ignored in schools.[11]

There are a number of reasons why we cannot escape this need for practical learning. Unless the learner practises there is no guarantee (to himself as well as others) that he understands what is required in performing a skill, particularly if this is related to a complicated object – the stripping down and re-assembly of a piece of machinery, for example. There is inevitably something excluded from even the best of descriptions and demonstrations. The schoolboy watching his craft teacher working on materials with tools may notice all the physical movements involved, but there are some things pertinent to skilled performance which he cannot know until he tries himself; the sharpness of tools, the hardness or plasticity of materials. The teacher may use words like hard, soft, sharp, pliable. But these are relative terms and their meaning in a given context can only be understood in practice. Even with the same tool at different times and with similar materials on different occasions there are slight differences which constitute an unexpected and, therefore, unspecifiable element. Dewey underlined this point in suggesting that 'undergoing' is the correlate of 'trying': 'We do something to the thing and it does something to us in return.'[12]

Thus, however specific a practitioner may be in analysing and explaining his skills, there remains what Polanyi calls 'a tacit component'.[13] At the heart of every skill there is something which remains unspecifiable: some particulars remain ineffable. In motor skills the tacit component consists mainly of 'touch'. Whether it is playing the piano, making a cover drive or man-handling a bale of cotton, skilled performance is ultimately a matter of the adjustment of the organism to the resistance of the object; partly a matter of pressure (literally touch), partly a question of timing. It is having the 'knack' and this, familiarly, is incommunicable. It is the mystery at the core of the craft which the learner must discover for himself. This element of mystery can be overplayed and used to excuse disregard of theory and precept. Though something crucial to a skill may elude specification, efficient technical education depends upon as much analysis and formulation of principle as possible. But in the end, making a skill one's own – having personal knowledge of it – and performing economically, comfortably, powerfully, 'perfectly', depends upon practice, upon first-hand experience, upon doing. And this is no less necessary for skills which are intellectual, social or professional in character than it is for manual skill. If one is to use concepts or principles correctly these must be refined by employing them experimentally in a variety of contexts.

It is this essential role of practice in the mastery of different kinds of skill which largely justifies the assumption that all learning is self-learning and that no one can really teach anyone else. In the end the teacher must hand over the initiative to the pupil. The assimilation, the structuring of material within his own existing conceptual framework is a function of the learner's own mental activity. On the other hand, it can by no means be taken for granted that the learner will be prepared to accept the responsibility for his own learning activities. Frequently he is unwilling to practice, to try things for himself. This is essentially the truth underlined by that well-worn educational metaphor, 'you can lead a horse to water but cannot make it drink'.[14] Just as the horse may stubbornly refuse to take in nourishment, so the child may refuse to practice. In the last resort it all depends on the child and many children (probably all children on occasion) clearly think the effort not worthwhile. But having conceded the necessity of the learner trying for himself and the possibility that there may be a refusal to try, one is not thereby committed to the view that in equally fundamental ways education must not be teacher-initiated. Indeed, there is a danger that to diminish the teacher's influence in education is itself a threat to the freedom and integrity of the child. Whilst recognizing the limitations of many traditional teaching activities, the importance of problem-solving and learning through practice as well as through theoretical explanations, it is important to turn and consider how far and in what sense the education of the child depends upon initiatives from the teacher.

REFERENCES

1   C. R. ROGERS *On Becoming a Person*, p. 276. Constable, London, 1961.
2   F. FROEBEL *The Education of Man*, p. 7. Edward Arnold, London, 1887.
3   J. PIAGET *Language and Thought of the Child*, p. 11.
4   I. SCHEFFLER *The Language of Education*, p. 68.
5   J. DEWEY *How We Think*, pp. 13–14.
6   J. DEWEY *Democracy and Education*, pp. 154–5.
7   G. H. BANTOCK *Education in an Industrial Society*, p. 33. And see HARDIE *Truth and Fallacy in Educational Theory*, p. 21.
8   R. S. PETERS 'Education as Initiation' in ARCHAMBAULT (Ed.) *Philosophical Analysis and Education*, p. 103.
9   JERSILD and others *Children's Interests*
10 E. BLISHEN (Ed.) *The School That I'd Like*, p 73 Penguin Books, 1969.
11 I have explored this problem at greater length in a paper

'Practical and Theoretical Learning' *British Journal of Educational Studies*, Vol. XVII, No. 2.

12   J. DEWEY *Experience and Education.*

13   See POLANYI *Personal Knowledge.*

14   See ROGERS, op. cit., and SCHOENCHEN *The Activity School*, p. 217.

9: *The teacher as agent of child-centred education*

THE LIMITATIONS OF CHILD—CENTRED LEARNING METAPHORS

Attempts to characterize the child as a learner are a fruitful source of educational metaphor. According to Scheffler,[1] metaphors 'often expose significant and surprising truths'. He also takes it for granted that the analogy between education and the content of the metaphor will break down at a certain point: 'every metaphor is limited in this way giving only a certain perspective on its subject'. Scheffler's remedy for this shortcoming is to employ a number of complementary metaphors. The naturalist's growth or plant metaphor insufficiently recognizes the cultural influence of the child's environment (see p. 100 above). It must be supplemented by the moulding or shaping metaphor which emphasizes the initiatives open to adults in selecting for the child those experiences which help to form his particular tastes and dispositions. In turn, the art metaphor remedies the defects of the moulding metaphor, since the sculptor, for example, cannot shape the marble irrespective of the internal structure of the stone. But though materials have their own natures and structures which cannot be ignored by the artist, they do not grow or develop spontaneously, and coming full circle, the plant metaphor emphasizes the child's inherent capacity for *growth* irrespective of interference from outside. However, the trouble with this corrective view of educational metaphors is that those who are emotionally committed to the sentiments contained in the growth metaphor are unlikely to see much merit in the moulding metaphor and vice versa. For, in terms of their appeal to the emotions, metaphors do not differ significantly from slogans: both tend to function as

battle cries, and to concede that one's adversary has a point is
to betray the cause.

In fact, it is difficult to see what learning metaphors can do for
educational theory that direct analyses of children's behaviour
in educational situations could not do a great deal better. It is
arguable that our educational theories would be sharper instruments, less liable to fallacy, if we could dispense with metaphors
altogether. But if our inability to transcend the concrete is such
that we must resort to this kind of simple picture language, one
way of doing justice to the complexity of the educational situation would be to develop these analogies much further than is
often the case. Arguably, the limitation of much metaphor-based
educational theory is best demonstrated not by allowing the
small nub of truth which metaphors reveal, but by developing
their implications a good deal further. To elaborate even child–
centred metaphors may be to point to a more active role for the
teacher in the child's education than is often apparent from the
surface of the analogy.

As well as emphasizing that only the learner himself can
appropriately assimilate educational experiences, the horse
and water metaphor (see p. 153 above) also helps to reinforce
the point that often the child has very little appetite for the
cultural menu offered by the school. So just as the horse must
really be thirsty if he is to drink, the child must be adequately
motivated if he is to learn. But this metaphor also acknowledges
that you can *lead* the horse to water. Implicitly, the animal might
be thirsty but incapable of knowing where to go to assuage his
thirst. Thus, this nourishment type of metaphor can be developed
to characterize the teacher's initiative as a leader in the educational situation. Where the horse and water metaphor really
breaks down is in face of the very limited range of food and
drink avilable to the horse. If we must discuss education by
comparing learning with the activity of nourishing a living
organism, we ought to focus upon the educational comparisons
implicit in the much greater variety of diet available to the
human animal. People practise gastronomy: the business of
supplying nourishment can be raised to the level of an art.
And conceived as *maître d'hôtel*, the teacher takes on a much

more creative role than when viewed (as is implicit in the horse and water metaphor) merely as ostler or stable boy.

To insist therefore that only the horse can drink and, implicitly, that only the child himself can decide to learn is not to establish that appetites cannot be stimulated by the sort of dish which is offered. We speak of 'whetting appetites' and the immature palate is not aware of what tastes it might develop. The teacher may have to stimulate an appetite sated by a diet of fudge. There can also be malnutrition and the child's uncultivated appetites may dispose him towards a 'candy-floss', chips-with-everything kind of diet which could be a threat to health. In educational terms, there is no reason to suppose that just as the child's spontaneous gastronomic dispositions may threaten his physical health, so his self-activated learning may not leave him intellectually undernourished or culturally impoverished. In this connection it is worth emphasizing the distinction (implicit at a number of points in this discussion) between *learning* and *learning in an educational situation* (see pp. 84–9, 123–4, 130, 141). Mere learning may be miseducative or normatively neutral and the child's own spontaneous learning may be in search of nourishment which is morally, culturally or physically at odds with his well-being: hence our emphasis upon the teacher as mediator of activities which are culturally valuable (see Chapter 5). Earlier, we took the view that individual appetites ought not to be indulged at the expense of a balanced educational diet (see Chapter 2). This assumption requires the Herbartian conclusion that 'instruction alone can lay claim to cultivate a balanced all-embracing many-sidedness'.[2] Herbart himself invoked the notion of cultural malnutrition to justify the teacher's deliberate and calculated initiatives in education: 'it is no wonder, when the mental diet is determined more by chance than by human skill, that a robust health, which can bid defiance to unfavourable influences, cannot always flourish on fare that is so often meagre'.[3] Jersild's investigation of children's interests underpinned this insight that interests may be taught as well as caught: 'to a large degree children's interests are learned. What a child likes to do is influenced by what he has an opportunity to like to do'. He noted a strong interest in music in a school where this was particularly well taught.[4] As with our physical appetites, cultural interest may be nourished in things for which we feel no imperative need but which enlarge perspectives and enhance the quality of life.

A positive and creative conception of the teacher's function can also be derived by development of another metaphor favoured by some Piagetians.[5] These stress the importance of the child's self-activity through the notion that he himself must build his own mental structure from the bricks of his daily experience. But though the child may be a builder, it is difficult to see him as architect of his own development. The initiative in this designing and planning function must lie with the adult. The building metaphor also suggests a positive function for the teacher which lies at the conclusion of the learning process. When the child has learned something the teacher has a responsibility to evaluate the resulting structure: is the building safe and fit for human habitation? There is a contemporary tendency to diminish the importance of the correct answer or the fact that one mode of learning may be technically preferable to others. In some curriculum areas – the arts, for example – objective criteria of assessment may be difficult to come by and it can be plausibly argued that since one man's meat is another man's poison, any child's creative activity is as good or valuable as any other's. But this argument cannot apply to mathematics and and in science, history and geography there are well-attested facts which it would be foolish to dispute or neglect. Especially when the learner is at a stage of *precision* (see Appendix) – when he is at grips with the 'grammar' of a subject – there are correct answers and the teacher abdicates his responsibility in failing to insist upon standards of accuracy and appropriate attention to detail. As well as architect or planner, the teacher functions in an evaluatory capacity, much as a clerk of works or local authority building inspector.

If the teacher is available as consultant in the design and evaluation of learning, how far is the child really quite alone when, having decided to eat, drink, build, travel or explore, he is actually embarked upon the learning process? As well as introducing children to appropriate learning situations – serving the dish, drawing the plans – one function of the teacher lies in indicating to the learner the structure of the field in which he wishes to learn. The recitation (as Dewey calls the traditional chalk and talk lesson) in school and the lecture in higher education can be valuable methods of reviewing the structure of a field of knowledge in order to show what might be learned and what problems the situation poses. The lecture or recitation is not so much an authoritarian situation as an opportunity for authorities to indicate the structure of a discipline; what has already been discovered, what other authorities believe. This is no more a matter of forcing 'inert ideas' upon unwilling learners than providing a tourist with a map on which places of interest are indicated is compelling him to go anywhere at all. Direct teaching of material by lecture or recitation can be the guide book situation. Or, as Ogden and Richards put it: 'A person thoroughly acquainted with his subject and with the techniques of definition should be able, like the man up aloft in the maze, to direct travellers from all quarters to any desired point; and it may be added that to go up the ladder and overlook the maze is by far the best method of mastering a subject.'[6] Self-education, if it is to have a sense of direction is, first, a matter of getting a panoramic view of the field. The short cuts, the well-trodden paths, the culs-de-sac, the length of the road, the resting places, the overnight stops, the filling stations and wayside inns are all worth knowing in advance. Hence, the teacher's function as a guide operates in relation to method as well as to content. In learning for themselves, students require not only some indication of the topography of the field, but also guidance on how to set about exploring it in the most economical and profitable way. For it is often both uneconomical and inefficient to pick things up for oneself. We often erect unnecessarily low and inconvenient ceilings to our competence in skills through a failure to seek appropriate expert help when we insist upon picking things up for ourselves. Those who teach themselves to type usually live to regret the limit upon speed and accuracy imposed by their early 'one finger exercises'. It is quite common and wise for people to seek guidance on how to tackle the learning of a skill before they embark upon it. And this seeking of advice is not always a matter of the helpless wanting to be *told* how to proceed, but of the intelligent learner interested in the pros and cons of different ways of setting about a task. Consulting this sort of advice may help to avoid the formation of bad habits which are often acquired in the process of picking up a skill for oneself and which have to be unlearned (a process often more difficult than learning) if efficiency is to be achieved.

Given that the child has to build his own mental framework from the materials of his environment, teaching him is a matter of arranging the pieces for him in such a way that their connections and relationships are readily discerned: or, like the clerk of works, of ensuring that the appropriate materials are ready and available at the proper time. This helpful supplying and arranging of materials is a matter of mediating – through the spoken word, books, documents, other physical objects – appropriate aspects of the environment so that the child encounters the parts in a sequence which makes it possible to discover meanings, discern patterns and build reliable intellectual structures. Thus, it may be a matter of giving him some materials but denying him others; of arranging for him to read texts in a particular order or in connection with other experiences. And the telling of which teaching sometimes undoubtedly consists is also this kind of activity. It rarely involves telling the learner all that is known to be the case; nor does it necessarily begin at the beginning and move, logically, step by step to the end. It is usually presenting selected items of information in relation to each other or to other experiences (looking at maps, reading descriptions, handling rocks, using tools, observing scientific experiments, taking nature walks etc.) so that the structuring, which the learner must himself initiate (in the sense of agreeing to drink) and organize can take place. The learner must himself set his learning in motion, but he will be unable to begin unless he discerns some pattern and knows how to begin and where to proceed.

Learners' evaluations of their own teachers are an indication that they do welcome teaching as an active function. Not merely are they conscious that interest in a subject or author or idea derives from the inspiration of some teacher: attitudes of mind, modes of thought, methods of study and ways of tackling a problem can each be traced to a particular teacher's influence. And if this suggests a teacher's example or inspiration rather than a more active intention on his part to set out deliberately to teach something, learners are conscious of subtleties of subject matter which confounded them until some teacher deliberately clarified the issue. 'Mr Smith makes things clear', 'I never understood that until Miss Brown explained it', 'Mr Jones shows you how to do it' – these phrases record the grateful pupil's indebtedness to the good teacher. Teachers are all too familiar with the fact that children may not bother to listen, look, or think; or that, trying hard, they nevertheless fail to grasp what is being taught. But equally, learners know that what was chaotic and meaningless gathers shape as a result of a teacher's intervention: that what they were *set* to learn does, in the perspective of time, often assume greater cultural value than what they have picked up for themselves. The quality of teaching as a contributory variable in pupil achievement is often overlooked in our obsession that test results should conform to some *a priori* notion of a normal distribution. It is worth asking whether the member of an educational conference quoted by Bruner was entirely deluding himself when he claimed: 'when you teach well it always seems as if seventy five per cent of the students are above the median'.[7] It is only to be regretted that students are grateful to teachers who clarify what is to be learned, on the grounds that such teachers have really provided crutches when they ought merely to have insisted upon the child's mastering the difficulty on his own.

TEACHERS OR TEACHING MACHINES?

Whatever legitimate initiatives may have been open to the teacher in the past, it seems to some educationists that the development of educational technology must considerably diminish his role in the future. Against the notion that teaching is an art – that the teacher functions creatively in responding to the novel situations which confront him daily in the classroom – there grows the idea that the invention of teaching machines makes him redundant. The learner's interests seem best served by mechanization of the educational process. In the mechanized classroom it appears that the teacher's role should approximate to that of a semi-skilled mechanic. As an American educationist observes, 'Radical advocates of what has been called the technological revolution in education seem to look forward to the time when they can say, "Goodbye, Mr Chips, and good riddance".'[8] Nor is this merely an American reaction. It is sometimes argued that the treasured freedom of the teacher in England is the product of historical accident, something of no intrinsic merit and potentially despotic, even capricious in its implications.[9] One writer representing the Association for Programmed Learning has demanded 'a complete school course in several subjects' programmed for use in simple machines and 'able to teach the student efficiently at his own pace, with minimum help from a qualified teacher'.[10] In this quotation the word 'complete' and the absence in its context of any reference to what the qualified teacher's function might be, other than as provider of 'minimum help', makes it not unreasonable to infer that in this kind of educational régime the teacher is expected to abdicate his creative function and assume the role of ancillary to the machine.[11] Nor is this merely the ideal of those outside the schools who have economic interests in educational technology. For example, Carl Rogers' strictures upon teaching are accompanied by a eulogy of teaching machines.[12]

In the face of these attacks upon the teacher, not all of his apprehension about the consequences of mechanizing education follows from selfish concern for loss of his own freedom and status. Teachers fear, simply but logically, that with the introduction of teaching machines education will become mechanical, and rote learning, a casualty of the child-centred movement, will return to classrooms with the machines. In one respect, this fear that machines threaten the meaningful learning situation seems unfounded. Indeed, it is often claimed that teaching machines are a child-centred device since one of their merits lies in facilitating that individualization of the learning process which we earlier identified as an important component of child-centred educational theory (see Chapter 2). As Stolurow puts it, teaching machines and programmed instruction are important in promoting the 'transition from mass education of individuals to individual education of the masses'.[13] Programmed instruction is assumed to individualize education in two important respects. First, the learner is freed from the inhibiting circumstances of parading his ignorance publicly; unlike the class lesson, the programmed situation has a comforting privacy: 'There is no embarrassing class of onlookers to observe mistakes, not even a teacher who might show disapproval'. Moreover, the pressures of the 'rat race' are removed: 'A student is competing with himself'.[14] The momentum of his learning can be accelerated or reduced without inviting invidious comparisons. The slow learner is not left irretrievably behind. Indeed, the notion of falling behind is inappropriate in this context. Since no one is setting the pace, there is no one to fall behind. This possibility of self-paced learning is the second sense in which programmed learning tends towards the individualization of education.

A further merit of programmed instruction is that it contributes to the precision of learning more effectively than the hard pressed teacher. A good programme will probably explore and teach the conceptual relationships inherent in a subject, concentrating on significant detail and imposing the discipline and drill of learning in a way few teachers can. Whatever their ability to analyse subject matter and to define the epistemological priorities involved in learning, teachers rarely have the time (caught up as they are in the insistent daily clamour of the school) to develop the insights into the structure of knowledge which an experienced programmer achieves. Precisely because he is unconcerned with flesh and blood and the limitations of a particular time and place, the programmer can analyse and programme data with a single-minded attention to detail which may elude the hard pressed teacher. Indeed, on the likely assumption that economic considerations will prevent the rapid mechanization of schools, one salutary effect of the contemporary stress on programmed learning may be in bringing home to teachers just how little attention they often pay to relevant detail.

However, at the precision stage of learning when the learner is committed to mastery of detailed material, it matters little whether he pores individually over exercise and textbooks or is confined in isolation with a machine. It is true that a machine may function as a romance device: much is made of the motivational value of the child's having a machine to operate himself. But as the novelty diminishes and machines become a commonplace in the classroom, one suspects that the reluctant learner will be no more willing to submit to the discipline of the machine than to that of the teacher: the drill which it enforces may be neither more nor less acceptable than the impositions of the teacher. And privacy in the educational situation has dangers which have to be set against its benefits. The possibility of the child being able to pace his own learning through the machine is a two-edged weapon: it is not always in the child's interest that he should be left to idle through his learning at his own pace.[15]

Moreover, quite as important as the fact that the learner has an individual speed is the fact that he has an individual strategy for solving problems, born of his unique experience and the peculiar combination of his interests and talents. But, as Janowitz and Street observe, not only is there a standardization of instruction implicit in mass produced (if economic) programmes which mocks at claims for individualization of learning; pressures are also exerted against the development of problem-solving skill since 'such individualisation as the new media provide may be almost wholly limited to informational learning'.[16] As Whitehead insisted (see Appendix), together with a precision stage of learning characterized, in part, by the mastery of information, romance and generalization are also vital components of the educational cycle. It is at a stage of romance, when learning must focus upon children's experiences, interests, concerns and aspirations as persons, and at a stage of generalization when they apply what they have mastered, that the teacher finds his opportunity to teach creatively. It is necessarily a characteristic of commercially produced educational programmes (one they share with most textbooks) that their concrete illustrative materials must be understandable irrespective of time and place. Programmes designed with the economic virtues of being saleable as widely and as long as possible must

The teacher as agent of child-centred education

inevitably wear a culturally neutral complexion. Exemplar situations cannot be drawn from the learner's own novel experience or his peculiar environment, nor can application or generalization be referred to the solution of problems of personal, topical or local concern. In the valid sense in which we earlier suggested that education should draw its data from life (see pp. 89–92), teaching programmes cannot capitalize upon the illustrative power of the changing scenes of life, unless they are prepared and revised frequently by the child's own teacher. Life-links of this sort can be forged only by teachers in daily contact with learners, aware of their distinctive interests, dispositions, problems and concerns.

As well as requiring a creative teacher-child relationship in this sense of catching and capitalizing the passing hour, good education is a social process. It is not merely that good teachers point the life relevance of what is learned, but that they lead and encourage conversation about its implications. Individual children often make contributions to oral lessons which are more than mere correct responses to set questions: in the dialectic of the classroom 'new' knowledge is discovered. This does not mean that major or significant novel contributions to human knowledge are made. But not infrequently, children contribute towards discussion from their own experience and illumine lesson material for themselves and others. Even the teacher learns from this socializing of the educational situation: it is within the experience of most teachers that they see subject matter in a new light from the response it evoked with a particular class. Hence, other values are explored, other attitudes are examined, other facts are seen to be relevant than those which the teacher (or programme or textbook) offer to learners for their consideration. There is a meeting of minds which is impossible when the inquiring mind of the learner encounters the inflexible 'mind' of the programme. Alternative paths in programmes only serve to bring the learner back to the one correct answer. Stolurow writes of programmed instruction being 'based upon a psychological analysis of the teaching-learning process as it takes place through the use of an educational dialogue between teacher and student'.[17] But it is an odd sort of dialogue which allows only for pre-packed responses as against the manifold possible reactions available to the teacher who has intimate knowledge of a particular child or class: the dialogue with the machine is rather like talking with the man who persists in contributing to a conversation as though he regards his companion's remarks as irrelevant interruptions to his own train of thought. The concept of prepared materials, sufficient in themselves rather than merely resources available to teachers, is inimical to those fruitfully contingent classroom interactions which follow from the teacher knowing the individual child: 'When it comes to the personalisation of learning – as contrasted with the individualisation of such things as learning rate, materials and feedback – machines, even those that only exist in the dreams of inventors, do not begin to compete with the human teacher.'[18] As Jackson also observes in a different context, 'Much of the teacher's effective knowledge as he goes about his work consists of idiosyncratic information about the particular set of students with whom he deals. Thus, the teacher may help to preserve the student's sense of personal identity by responding to him as a person, not just as a role incumbent'.[19] From a recent publication presenting the views of children on their ideal school, it is clear that whatever lack of enthusiasm they often display for their teachers, 'they would not want them replaced by machines'. So far as children's preferences in this matter should be an item in our assessment of the case for mechanization of the school, it is significant that these children 'couldn't imagine circumstances in which a teacher might be replaced by a machine; teachers were of enormous importance to them'.[20]

All this is to argue that the skilled practitioner must be in a continuous face-to-face relationship with the learner, committed to the task of helping him towards personal knowledge and skill by pointing its relevance and meaning in terms of his own powers and limitations. For it is evident that the weaknesses of learners are not always such that they can be solved by merely altering the pace at which learning occurs. The variety of personal and sociological factors which inhibit learning and the complex of factors affecting an individual's motivation are such that the participation of someone who knows the child personally seems essential to the educational situation.

Those who find it difficult to take seriously the concept of teaching as an art are often worried about the possibility of recruiting sufficient entrants to the teaching profession with the personal and cultural resources to forge this creative relationship between themselves and children. Whilst agreeing that artistry characterizes the work of a relatively few good practitioners, they see the average teacher as distinguished, at best, only by his mediocrity. Enthusiasm for the mechanization of schooling often conceals a mistrust of the average teacher which is nowadays rarely as candidly expressed as it was by Pestalozzi, himself a central figure in the child-centred tradition. Indeed, Pestalozzi would not have felt out of place in a world of teaching machines. He displayed a similar disregard for the creative role of the teacher to that currently displayed by some enthusiasts for programmed learning, believing that in early education the teacher ought to be a mere cipher. A good teaching method should be foolproof and compensate for the shortcomings of the indifferent teacher: 'I believe that it is not possible for common popular instruction to advance a step, so long as formulas of instruction are not found which make the teacher, at least in the elementary stages of knowledge, merely the tool of method, the result of which springs from the nature of the formulas and not from the skill of the man who uses it.'[21] Pestalozzi's mistrust of the teacher differed somewhat from that of those who suspect his authoritarianism and fear that teaching may distort the child's nature or diminish his capacity for creative activity. He simply could not trust other teachers to understand the educational situation or to develop a personal methodology. For in his view, efficient education depended upon discovering *the* method, not on sensitizing teachers to the strengths and limitations of individual children. Throughout Pestalozzi's work there runs the conviction that he has found the uniquely appropriate educational method. And the point is not that his method has characteristics which strike us today as exceedingly formal so that we are inclined to dismiss it as the wrong method: the fact is that *the* method is an educational will o' the wisp. The process of education requires a nice balance between the fortuitous and the intentional, the deliberate and the haphazard. This follows from the fact that we learn from the whole of our environment and not just from the school. We bring to our schooling different qualities and kinds of experience and our opportunities to apply what we learn outside the school are equally varied. Much of what the teacher does is opportunist in character. Part of his artistry lies in his ability to capitalize upon the educative possibilities of his own scholarship and knowledge and those children's life experiences which the contingencies of their daily contact in the classroom throw into fruitful juxtaposition. Even in a skill like learning to read where it might appear that orders of procedure could be prescribed with some certainty, research into this problem suggests that the efficacy of one method over another is not an absolute thing so much as relative to the competence and disposition of the particular teacher.[22] This is really the point about Pestalozzi's method. What one gathers from his educational writing is not that he has a method of universal validity, but that one is witnessing a teacher at work who succeeded because of what he was as a person having unique gifts. The impression made upon his associates and the enthusiasm, conviction and *élan* which shine from every page, these rather than the liberality or appropriateness of the method are what impress upon the reader that he is watching the work of a teacher of genius.

However, it would be unrealistic to pretend that most of us who teach are able to bring even a tithe of Pestalozzi's gifts to the daily business of teaching. It would even be folly to contend that a body the size of the teaching profession consisted entirely of satisfactory practitioners: the poor or mediocre teacher does constitute a threat to children. The provision of educational aids may do something to mitigate this problem. But the bureaucratization of teaching (as when the teacher's role and function is largely determined for him by the standardization of teaching programmes which diminish the possibility of creative decision-making) may, in removing one kind of impediment to sound education, throw up others: 'To the extent that the new media increase centralization of authority, contribute to inflexibility in curriculum, and heighten a loss of professional autonomy, they will be self-perpetuating and even more difficult to cope with than the old fashioned modes of standardisation.'[23] Moreover, it is not even certain that educational technology will make good the deficiencies of the unsatisfactory teacher: experience suggests that the poor unimaginative teacher produces the same educational travesty from mechanical aids as he does with any conventional educational resource. Perhaps, ultimately, it is possible to envisage schools in which the 'teachers' – those in minute-by-minute contact with children – are technicians charged merely with the duty of setting up and maintaining educational materials to the requirements of children whose individual curricula are programmed in the computerized 'control room' of the school (or in the educational 'service station' as such an educational conception is sometimes aptly named). That such impersonalization of learning and teaching would be anathema to most educationists ought not to deter us from a dispassionate evaluation of the merits of this sort of Utopianism. But since the economics of even the most affluent of societies makes such a capital intensive approach to education a very remote possibility, discussion of its desirability need not detain us here. In fact, most highly industrialized, high income societies are currently engaged in reforms designed to extend the period of professional education for teachers. They are committed to the faith that whatever the innovations in educational technology, teachers must be better cultivated and more resourceful in seizing educational initiatives in a changing world than they have ever been before. And this extension of the period of teacher education would represent a wastage of scarce social resources if the idea of the teacher as a creative innovator were merely a sacred cow as ripe for slaughter as some over-zealous advocates of educational technology would have us believe. However, there is a well established myth that the educated teacher is himself a threat to good education. Thus, at this point, it is appropriate to consider the implications for the education of the child of current attempts to improve teacher training.

REFERENCES

1 I. SCHEFFLER *Language and Education*, Ch. 3.
2 HERBART *The Science of Education*, p. 141.
3 HERBART, op. cit., p. 79.
4 JERSILD AND OTHERS *Children's Interests*, p. 37.
5 See, for example, N. ISAACS *The Growth of Understanding in the Young Child*, pp. 12–14. Educational Development Association, 1961.
6 C. K. OGDEN and I. A. RICHARDS *The Meaning of Meaning*, p. 216. Kegan Paul, Trench & Trubner, London, 1923.
7 BRUNER *The Process of Education*, p. 9.
8 P. W. JACKSON *The Teacher and the Machine*, p. 3. University of Pittsburgh Press, 1968.
9 See, for example, F. MUSGROVE and P. TAYLOR 'The New Despots', *Sunday Times*, 9 March 1969, for an analysis of some implications of the English teacher's freedom. This is an advanced summary of their book, *Society and the Teacher's Role*, to be published by Routledge & Kegan Paul, London.
10 Letter in *New Society*, 26 October 1962. See also the editorial 'Freedom from What in the Classroom?' in *New Society*, 1 November 1962.
11 However, some advocates of programmed learning are more circumspect in seeing teaching machines only as substitute teachers in areas where teacher supply falls short of demand (e.g., in meeting the deficiencies of mathematics teachers in girls' schools). See, for example, H. KAY in K. AUSTWICK (Ed.) *Teaching Machines and Programming*, pp. 4–5. Pergamon Press, Oxford, 1964.
12 ROGERS *On becoming a Person*, p. 294.
13 L. M. STOLUROW 'Programmed Instruction and Teaching Machines' in P. H. ROSSI and B. J. BIDDLE (Eds.) *The New Media and Education*, Aldine Publishing Co., Chicago, 1966. See also AUSTWICK, op. cit., p. 175; J. I. TABA and others *Learning and Programmed Instruction*, Ch. I, Addison-Wesley, Reading, Mass., 1965; Editor's introduction in M. GOLDSMITH (Ed.) *Mechanisation in the Classroom*, Souvenir Press, London, 1963.
14 KAY, op. cit., p. 39.
15 See JACKSON, op. cit., pp. 34–51, for an extended criticism

of the claim that educational technology intensifies the individualization of education.

16 M. JANOWITIZ and D. STREET in Rossi and Riddle, op. cit., who note the tendency to concentrate on the 'communication effects' of the new media to the neglect of attempts to assess their side-effects in terms of the long-term impact upon student and teacher morale.

17 STOLUROW, loc. cit.

18 P. W. JACKSON *The Teacher and the Machine*, p. 46.

19 P. W. JACKSON *Life in Classrooms*, p. 152.

20 See BLISHEN (Ed.) *The School that I'd Like*.

21 PESTALOZZI *How Gertrude Teaches Her Children*, p. 41.

22 L. A. REID *Philosophy and Education*, p. 43, quoting Wall. With reference to reading, for which Pestalozzi did believe he had found a foolproof teaching method, see G. R. ROBERTS *Reading in Primary Schools*, Routledge & Kegan Paul, London, 1969. In Chapter 8, Roberts stresses the limitations of methods aside from their employment by skilled and understanding teachers and cites research to the effect that 'actual reading methods . . . matter far less than the manner and skill with which they are employed, and other attributes of the teacher concerned'.

23 JANOWITIZ and STREET, op. cit.

10: Teacher training and child-centred education

The belief that the teacher's own education may be a threat to the child is not uncommon even among educationists. The two recent major developments in the education of English teachers – the three-year course of training and the establishment of the degree of B.Ed. – have had a mixed reception from the teaching profession. As a step towards improved professional status they have been welcomed. But to some teachers it is by no means evident that these reforms have been implemented with the best interests of children in mind.

In particular there is concern at what is taken to be the subsidiary place of the study of education (and practical teaching in the schools) in both these extended courses of training: 'There are grave misgivings that in some cases the degree is not biased towards education, but is, rather, a general type of degree in which education happens to be included.'[1] Child-centred educationists who emphasize the child as opposed to the subject are apt to favour teacher education strongly biased towards professional courses and practical teaching and to contend for a diminution of 'academic' content. This argument is advanced particularly on behalf of teachers of primary and less able secondary children. It is thought that we shall perform a disservice to these children by an emphasis upon academic models more appropriate to the demands of the grammar school: the more intending teachers are preoccupied with academic disciplines, the more their teaching is likely to be subject-centred. The myth persists that the highly educated cannot really teach and that provided the teacher knows the child, he can teach him from a shallow academic base. However, one of our conclusions – that educational disciplines ought to be viewed developmentally – might be taken to imply some degree of specialized teaching even in the primary school. Although this is at odds with current primary school practice of using the teacher as a general practitioner, a degree of specialization in primary education was implied in the writings of John Dewey over half a century ago and, more recently, in the Plowden Report. Dewey anticipated the notion (sometimes canvassed today but by no means a commonplace of educational thought) that the teacher of number in the primary school should be an educated mathematician: 'Really to interpret the child's present crude impulses in counting, measuring and arranging things in rhythmic series involves mathematical scholarship – a knowledge of the mathematical formulae and relations which have, in the history of the race, grown out of such crude beginnings.'[2] The problem of the 'scholar-teacher' implied in Dewey's prescription is complicated in the primary school by the non-specialist character which the teacher's work has traditionally assumed. Once the case for the teacher's having a scholarly competence is agreed, we are faced with the unreasonable expectation that the primary teacher needs to be an expert over the whole range of the curriculum. In the past, training institutions have attempted to help the teacher meet this need for comprehensive coverage of the whole curriculum by providing a variety of 'Curriculum Courses' of short duration.[3] However, it is debatable whether these short courses have really provided the teacher with much more than academic crutches.

Two other solutions to this problem seem possible: either we abandon the well entrenched assumption that the primary child needs to spend the whole of his school day throughout the year with the same teacher, thus making some degree of specialization possible; or we explore the notion of general teachers with specialist competencies, available as consultants to each other, perhaps functioning as teams of teachers led in each curriculum area by the staff's expert in that area. Both of these alternatives find sanction in the Plowden Report. The commissioners queried the assumption that the primary teacher must always be 'mother hen' believing that 'Even young children can work happily with more than one adult'.[4] They also noted and approved the existing practice of exchanging classes to capitalize on the special interests and competencies of individual teachers. The introduction of primary school French has been based largely upon specialized teaching and the development of team teaching is recommended as a method of ensuring that the child comes into contact with teachers 'having some mastery of the English subjects, of a modern language, of mathematics and science, and of the arts'.[5] In this respect, the recommendation to extend primary schooling by one year strengthens the case for some specialization in the upper classes of the 'middle school': 'The older children might benefit from a more systematically planned contact with two or three teachers, each expert in one of the main aspects of the curriculum and able to teach related subjects. As the range of the primary school curriculum widens, it becomes increasingly difficult to equip students in a three-year course to teach all subjects to older pupils.'[6] To this end the report reminds graduates that the schools need the specialist knowledge they can bring to primary education and promises that they, in turn, 'will find that it (the primary school) offers intellectually challenging work'.[7]

As well as fear for the primary school child, suspicion of an intensified academic education for teachers also stems from concern for the education of the 'non-academic' learner at all levels in schools. It is argued that the teacher of this sort of child is best equipped by deepening his understanding of children rather than extending his familiarity with academic subjects.

However, one's experience in teacher training suggests that whatever the age or ability group in question, and aside from the student teacher who is temperamentally incapable of keeping order in a class-room, teaching is often inadequate, not because the teacher doesn't know the children, but because he doesn't know enough of the history or geography or science he is being asked to teach (it is interesting that head teachers who value teachers who can teach children, not subjects, still organize the curriculum on traditional subject lines). In geography he has the names of towns, rivers, products, exports and imports, but often no grasp of the principles which underly these facts and

their relationships, and little knowledge of the human implications of living in a particular locality other than can be categorized under occupational headings. His geography is merely
'capes and bays' (which has its place in the curriculum) and often
out-dated economic statistics found in the geography textbook.
Or if he is teaching any one of the innumerable wars in human
history, he can draw maps of the campaigns, name the battles,
the participants, the treaties and their terms. But he often knows
little of the concrete detail required to bring out the drama,
tragedy, pathos and courage of war, and which contributes to an
imaginative understanding both of this particular historical
event and of the struggle of men, through time, to come to grips
with their environment and transcend its tragic implications.
The lesson introduction: 'We are going to talk about the Battle
of—' is usually greeted with gasps of eager anticipation from a
class of children, in contrast to the bored resignation with which
they eventually find themselves listening to a mere catalogue of
names, dates and places. One suspects that children can often
recite the causes of a war without any conception of the way in
which these were 'causes'. Dealing, for instance, with the
development of the Poor Law, the teacher narrates dates and
details of legislation and uses words like 'pauper' and 'workhouse' without conveying by reference to the circumstances of
the poor or conditions in the workhouse, anything of the
abhorrence in which the Poor Law was held by the working
classes until quite recently. He is familiar with the jargon of the
history textbook but the reports of poor, factory and educational
commissioners are, literally, closed books to him: not necessarily through any fault of his own, but because of the prevailing
atmosphere in which subject matter counts for little and which
encourages the pretence that it is easy enough to 'get up' all
that children need.

Now, it could be objected that these examples from history
and geography make the opposite point to that intended. Inexperienced teachers do not know the detail which would interest
the child. They have merely 'watered down' their college notes
or recited material as outlined in the textbook: they are simply
not child-centred enough. But it remains a fact that it is a

knowledge of subject matter which they lack. They are ignorant of the concrete human experiences and events which bring textbook history to life. The remedy in teacher education is to pay more attention to academic content, not less. No doubt critics fear that more work on so-called 'academic' subjects would only consist of more material to be watered down, more verbalism, more names to be dropped in front of uncomprehending pupils and nothing of the kind of concrete material likely to quicken the interest of children. But to express this fear really constitutes an argument against the wrong kind of academic course, not against acquisition of subject matter as such. And it is no remedy for school courses which are merely diluted adult courses to divert the student's attention from subject to child. Often enough his theoretical observations about teaching are impeccably child-centred. He knows what he ought to know of child development and of children's needs and interests and he knows which methods will make his teaching vital to the child. He teaches watered down material, not because he fails to understand children and thinks this is what they need, but because it is all he knows; it comes most readily to hand from the nearest available textbook. He often knows that what he is doing is not the most appropriate thing to do and he is a different teacher when working with material whose educational possibilities he more fully understands, because he knows it more thoroughly, has thought about it more acutely and has done his research into those aspects of it which bring concreteness to the abstractions he wants to teach.

This suggests that having better educated teachers requires an emphasis in teacher training upon acquiring a culture to communicate, rather than a movement towards greater stress upon professional studies. Nevertheless, it has to be recognized that fears about the educated teacher's difficulty in communicating with children involves a valid criticism of the nature of much traditional academic education of teachers. It is necessary to ask what conception of an academic discipline is pertinent to those who intend to teach it to others: and secondly, how far is the separation into 'academic' and 'professional' a useful conceptual instrument with which to approach teacher education?

The first of these problems is complicated by the peculiar circumstances of the college of education. Unlike the university (at the undergraduate level), it has to fulfil two functions whose requirements appear incompatible. It is a means towards furthering the personal education of the student as well as a professional training and, it is sometimes argued, the first of these ought not to be a means towards the second. In the past, the stress upon the importance of the student's personal education has prompted some Institutes of Education to adopt a policy of requiring a student's main academic course to be geared to personal rather than professional requirements; as though the teacher's personal culture were the least of the resources which he brings into the classroom. Subsidiary courses were designed to provide professional orientation, but a main course had to be devised to minister to the interests of the mature adult, without concession to the question of how it might be adapted to the requirements of children. However, in terms of its practical consequences this ignores student psychology. Those who have gone to teach in secondary schools where the curriculum is usually organized along specialist lines have, wisely, regarded their competence to specialize as falling within the area of their main college subject. This is what they know best and, they assume, what they can teach most authoritatively. But, paradoxically, this has often been the subject of their college course which has been studied without reference to its pedagogical implications. The subsidiary subject which has been set within the teaching context they know only superficially.

In discussing the content of the student's academic course, we ought to begin from the assumption that this will consist of subjects which he might wish to teach and that, whatever he decides to teach, he should have mastered it as an authority. So far as his ability and time permit, he should have come to grips with a subject area as a logically structured body of knowledge, as well as knowing how the abstractions with which it is concerned are related to concrete data within human experience. The Piagetian stress upon the need for experience of concrete operations prior to formal-operational thinking is widely accepted. And subject teaching is often inadequate, precisely

12

because it deals entirely with logical structures which are characteristic of formal operations.

Consequently, academic disciplines which students are likely to teach should be learned and known concretely. But this does not mean that subject courses in colleges of education must consist largely of trivia. One is not contending for an academic study of history, for example, in which the students acquire an encyclopaedic collection of anecdotes of the type 'Wolfe and Gray's Elegy', 'Alfred and the cakes' or 'the boyhood of Clive'. Biographical data must at least include that which constitutes the reasons why people are in the history books. For this reason, these 'romantic' scraps of information may be important – the myths of history are relevant to historical understanding no less than the accredited facts – but they by no means exhaust that concrete data which is relevant for the curriculum of even the less able child. As our earlier example of faulty history teaching indicated, concreteness in a subject like history is a matter of familiarity with sources. The reports of government commissioners and inspectors, letters, contemporary fiction, newspapers, architecture and industrial archaeology are the stuff out of which a scholarly study of history is made. These original sources also contain the sort of concrete data which brings history to life for children of all ages and abilities. Thus, if academic courses in higher education have the proper concrete reference which give abstractions meaning for the scholar, there should be no conflict between the requirements of a student's personal education and the knowledge he needs to teach his subject developmentally, bearing the educational needs of different age and ability groups in mind. I am aware that this assumption has only been argued with reference to history (but see also the comments about the developmental teaching of social disciplines in Chapter 5) with which, as a teacher, I am most familiar. It may not be possible to identify this congruence of the scholar's and the child's interest in other disciplinary areas but it seems worth the attempt. In higher education, no less than in schools, there is a danger that disciplines will be insufficiently concrete for the student's own proper understanding. As with children, there is a danger of students merely memorizing and parroting the high level generalizations of scholars. One has in mind the encouragement given to students (especially by some textbooks) to categorize philosophers, educational and political theorists under various -isms (Idealism, Pragmatism, Naturalism, Empiricism, Utilitarianism etc.) without their understanding what makes a thinker a Rationalist, say, or having the concept of Rationalism at a level which would enable them to identify another Rationalist if they met one. This danger will be minimized by ensuring that at any stage, and in any discipline, abstract learning is related to appropriate concrete data. In this connection it is useful to remember that the influential developmental psychology of Piaget does not imply a naïve child-centredness of the sort which holds subject matter of no importance. Most of Piaget's inferences about intellectual development are derived from observations of children's attempts to conceptualize their growing understanding of scientific concepts from distinctive areas of knowledge and experience. And their attainment of a formal-operational stage of intellectual development is signalled by their capacity to operate with concepts in a manner congruent with the logical operations of scholars in different academic fields.

A second factor which helps to perpetuate the antithesis between subject and child is the separation of college courses into 'academic' and 'professional'. One unfortunate consequence of this is that the roles of 'subject' and 'education' lecturers in colleges of education have often assumed an exclusiveness which not only reflects, but probably helps to perpetuate, the child-subject dichotomy. A further consequence is a lowering of the status of the subject 'Education'. The assumption that it is not 'academic' leads to the conclusion that it is not capable of sustaining rigorous, disciplined or scholarly study. In academic circles it is frequently overlooked that education has been an object of scholarly study since the Greeks. Few major figures in the history of Western thought have felt able to ignore the problem of how a civilization deliberately communicates its culture to the young, and many have produced works entirely or substantially devoted to education. In consequence there exists a considerable classical and modern literature of education. But a subject categorized as 'professional' inevitably carries some of the stigma which attaches in English education to studies which have a practical or vocational reference. However, here we are concerned with more than the semantic adjustment required to make Education respectable. The task of making school subjects meaningful for the child requires insights from both academic and educational studies. Here there is obviously ground for inter-disciplinary study. Those lecturers who are concerned with the teaching of a subject discipline and those whose pre-occupation is the nature of the educational process ought to find common ground in attempting to define what sort of entity the discipline in question really is: the logical status and inter-dependence of the facts, concepts and principles it embraces; the extent of its dependence upon data from other disciplines; the areas of human experience to which it has a concrete reference; its methodology and historical development; its character as an autonomous or a derived area of study; the essentially theo-retical or 'applied' nature of its explanations of phenomena, and, not least, the sorts of priorities involved in communicating its concepts, principles and skills to the learner. Whether, to achieve this objective of discovering exactly what a particular discipline is and how best to teach it, we create special courses or whether we do it within the subject or the Education courses is not important: existing interests of members of staff ('vested' as well as academic) will determine where the emphasis falls in any particular college. But there is no reason why the teacher of the subject and the 'special method' lecturer in the Education course should not be the same person. The unfortunate tendency for college staffs to fragment into education lecturers and subject lecturers might be avoided, and learning theory might gain in relevance to children's education, if the teaching of curriculum and method were primarily in the hands of subject lecturers. In educational psychology courses, learning theory often consists of a mountain of vague generalization which requires consider-able forcing in order to produce a mouse of a prescription relevant to the learning situation in the classroom. Hence, if the psychology of learning is to have educational relevance, it should derive its data and concepts from those situations in the classroom where children are set deliberately to acquire knowledge and skills from the different disciplines. Perhaps academic psychologists are not the best people, by training or by inclination, to undertake this re-orientation, a task that could be best undertaken by subject lecturers prepared to acquire the appropriate psychological training.

In this chapter the emphasis has been upon the importance of the teacher acquiring a culture to teach, if only because preoccupation with the 'children, not subjects' slogan has led to the devaluing of curriculum content in favour of studies of the child. Elsewhere we noted how the child-centred tradition has emphasized the importance of the teacher knowing *the child as an individual* (see Chapter 2), understanding the nature of his motivation *as a child* (see Chapter 5), and being conversant with the impediments to learning which can be imposed by the cultural limitations of family and neighbourhood (see Chapter 11), as well as the educational potential of the child's own experience of his environment. It is not sufficient for the teacher to be aware of the 'logical geography' of human knowledge and its epistemological priorities. The child does not learn in a cultural vacuum. Thus, there is the problem of the sociology of learning. How important is the cultural capital which the child brings to school? How does family, class, neighbourhood and geographical background affect the concepts he understands and the language he speaks? Will the concrete material used to illustrate principles already be part of his experience? (One recalls the expressions of incomprehension on the faces of lower working class children in an industrial city when a student teacher said, 'you know what happens when your *Daddy* writes a *cheque.*') What emotional predispositions does he bring to the task of learning? Will some of the barriers to his understanding be a product of his class or family background? Considerations of this kind help to define where the teacher has to meet the child and the sort of exemplar situations which will have meaning for him.[8] But as well as his general insights into the stages of child development and the sociological correlates of learning, the teacher needs to be sensitive to the *peculiar* qualities and limitations which the learner brings to the task. He is likely to share his cultural advantages or impediments with his fellows in the class, but other strengths and limitations are peculiarly his. It is in this diagnostic context that measurements of ability, achievement and aptitude become most relevant. The teacher is under an obligation to meet the learner as a mind with a history all its own. It is incumbent upon him to discover what quality of mind the learner brings to school, a product of his innate characteristics and his experience. Has he already mastered the steps, skills, concepts, principles and categories which are antecedent to the new learning he needs to undertake? Has he knowledge of the concrete instances from which complex concepts are derived? In the Piagetian terminology, has he still only the capacity for pre-operational or concrete operational thought? In attempting to answer questions of this sort the teacher develops a conception of what activity and experience the child is capable of, resulting from his immaturity (a condition he shares with other children of similar mental age) and from individual gifts or limitations.

It is this sort of knowledge about the nature of the learner within his cultural context which has formed the substance of education courses in psychology and sociology. Additional insights from wider cultural perspectives can be gained from study of the history of education (currently somewhat neglected by colleges) and comparative education (now growing in popularity). Conclusions about the capacities and interests of children exemplify a narrow parochialism when they are merely the product of a student's own exercise in child study. Just as the child's immediate environment is not always the most suitable from which to draw conclusions about the cultural experiences into which he might be initiated, so are the school situations in which some students study child behaviour unpromising for the development of an adequate educational theory. We must, at least, attend to what has been found educationally possible and desirable in other cultures and at other times. Moreover, since many of the problems of child-centred education are conceptual in character, students should be involved in philosophical discussion about the meanings which might be ascribed to the concepts of freedom, authority, discipline, wholeness, experience, environment, individual, social, preparation, life, when these are used in an educational context.

A fundamental difficulty in teacher training is that of the balance which ought to be achieved between subject and educational courses. The problem is one of relating 'academic' and 'professional' studies so that they focus upon the common question of how the child acquires knowledge and skill given his stage of development as a learner and the structure of human knowledge. In part, this problem of balance is related to the kind of institution in which a student intends to teach: different emphasis may be required to meet the differing conditions in primary and secondary education or in different types of secondary school. There may also be valid arguments against specialist concentration upon a single academic discipline. Social studies, for example, might best be taught by students whose own education is rooted in more than one of the social disciplines. Again, complaint about the traditional subject curriculum often focuses upon our fixation with classical modes of explaining reality and the difficulty of introducing newer disciplines concerned with the developing practical and theoretical interests of contemporary man. Curriculum construction must become more sensitive to these changing human interests, and colleges of education be prepared to widen their own curricula to meet changing emphases in the school. Too often the demand for introduction of new disciplines into schools is met with the response that there is no one equipped to teach them. In this connection, it is interesting that some of the published B.Ed. syllabuses give the impression that the curriculum ossified half a century ago. But given these problems of balance, and the difficulty of keeping college curricula fresh and responsive to the changing needs of the schools, the conclusions of this study give no warrant for the view that even in preparation for teaching which is child-centred, the importance of subject disciplines should be diminished in the education of teachers.

REFERENCES

1   G. PRICE 'The New Degree in Education' *Forum*, Vol. 10,

No. 1. See also the document *The B.Ed. Degree* issued on behalf of the Executive of the National Union of Teachers (1968), especially para. 7.

2 J. DEWEY *The Child and the Curriculum*, p. 17.

3 See Ministry of Education Pamphlet No. 34 *The Training of Teachers*. H.M.S.O., London, 1957.

4 Central Advisory Council for Education (England) *Children and Their Primary Schools* (Plowden Report), para. 769. H.M.S.O., London, 1967.

5 Plowden Report, paras. 761–8. It is interesting that the Newsom Report advocated the development of team teaching for similar reasons – see para. 288.

6 Plowden Report, para. 773.

7 Plowden Report, para. 965.

8 The Newsom Report (para. 103) stressed the importance of sociological understanding for all teachers in training, a reasonable requirement in view of its earlier focus on the impediments to learning imposed by the social environment of schools in parts of our large industrial cities (see pp. 190–4 below). See also E. HOYLE *The Role of the Teacher*, Ch. 2. Routledge & Kegan Paul, London, 1969.

11 : *Child-centred education in theory and practice*

The assumption is widespread among practising teachers that educational theory must lie on the other side of an unbridgeable gulf from classroom practice. And more than most educational prescriptions, those associated with the child-centred tradition are apt to be dismissed by practising teachers as good in theory but unworkable in practice.

One approach to this problem of the disjunction between theory and practice is to argue that it is our theories which must be inadequate if they are so far adrift from educational practice: there is not some mysterious metaphysical entity which prevents good theory from being related to successful practice. On this view, where the theory-practice gap exists, we ought to begin with a re-examination of theory. It is not a matter of devising some third bridging factor to enable us to straddle the gap, but rather one of acknowledging that our theories (often nothing more than pious slogans) have been shown to be defective.

An obvious reason for the defects in educational theory lies in our failure to distinguish sufficiently between different kinds and levels of theoretical explanation. Not merely do we often theorize as though we were educating in Utopia, but we often fail to acknowledge necessary distinctions between the different sorts of practical activity which characterize an educational system. The educational process requires a complex of decision-making at many different levels. The range extends from those decisions made by national governments about the administrative structure and the share of economic resources which are to be allocated to the different sectors of the system, to those quite different judgements made on the classroom floor about the way to teach reading or history, or the sort of punishment (if any) appropriate to the misdemeanors of a particular child. So far as the multitude of possible decisions which lie between these extremes are theory-based, they call on quite different modes of theoretical explanation. But often, for example, there is a tendency to ignore the distinction we drew in our introduction, and which has been employed at different points in this analysis, between technical or instrumental and categorical or moral prescriptions (see pp. 17–18); or hopes, dreams and aspirations are not distinguished from facts; the educational fantasies from the possibilities. Thus, a gap between theory and practice seems inevitable in the face of much Utopian theorizing which produces quite inappropriate and inapplicable educational models (sometimes from a failure simply to account for the limitations which the weaknesses of the flesh must impose upon 'the best laid schemes') and from a failure to distinguish the different sorts of explanation required by different kinds and levels of educational activity.

Sometimes, then, the theory-practice gap is a matter of our having unsatisfactory theory. But there is a sense in which it is impossible to bridge the gap if this means finding a 'one-to-one' correspondence between our theories and our practical activities. To expect this is to misunderstand the nature of theories and their relationship with practical activity. We miss the point of theorizing if we ever expect that any theory of the behaviour of men or natural phenomena will correspond in detail with any practical situation. Theories derive what usefulness they have from being generalizations – abstractions from particular situations.[1] They are relevant to all those practical situations which they seek to explain precisely because they are an accurate description of none. To gain relevance, theories have to be applied. This suggests that we often dismiss theory as irrelevant to practice because we are asking theories to perform tasks which, by their nature, they are unfitted to perform. The implications for teacher education of this necessary divergence of practice from theory has received scant attention from educational theorists and it is a theme which must lie outside the scope of this chapter. However, one ought, at least, to point to some of the features in the practical situation which exist to limit the application of such prescriptions as have emerged in the course of this analysis.

LIMITATIONS IMPOSED BY THE INSTITUTIONALIZATION OF EDUCATION

Even the conclusion that the child is the fundamental item in the educational nexus – that unless the pupil learns there is no educational situation – is by no means self-evident if we examine educational practice. Independent observers of the school situation could often be forgiven for concluding that educational institutions assume a life and momentum of their own, such that learners become an unwelcome intrusion. What is administratively convenient rather than what is educationally efficacious seems the governing consideration in some schools and colleges and is probably a factor in all educational institutions for some of the time. Schools are not unknown where the caretaker determines educational method. Modes of classroom organization which make life difficult or unpredictable for the cleaners are not tolerated and, from this standpoint alone, there is an administrative pressure towards a formally structured classroom organization. Much the same is true of procedures which threaten tidy timetabling. Yet it is characteristic of the informal methods which follow from stressing freedom, individualism, or the child as initiator of his own learning, that these are often difficult to assimilate within the established organizational patterns of schools.

This sort of practical impediment to the implementation of theory can also be illustrated by reference to the problem of securing a present orientation to schooling. The protest against preparation as an educational aim (see Chapter 5) rarely stems from a failure to recognize the legitimate claims of the child's future: it is more likely to be a polemic against those pressures which frustrate attempts to use the present aspirations and interests of children as points of departure for the educational enterprise. Earlier, we attempted to resolve this present-future antithesis by taking a developmental view of the curriculum as the necessary correlate of developmental learning theory. But a thoroughgoing developmental conception of education which insists upon meeting the child where he is, which seeks exemplification of material from his own experience and caters for his own talents and limitations is particularly vulnerable to bureaucratic pressures. For example, the teacher faces the problem of filling the school day throughout the school year. Timetables often take little account of present capacity for growth and understanding. Present need and interest may demand that the child is anywhere but in school today: at the zoo, climbing trees, visiting grandfather, burying grandmother and so on. Or, in terms of his capacity to assimilate schooling, the child's educational needs might be adequately met by his attendance at school for only part of the day. Yet not only are there inelastically prescribed times for attendance at school and legislation against persistent absenteeism, but also, once the child is in school, the teacher stands to the child *in loco parentis* and schools are often much more punctilious than parents in providing supervision whilst children are in their care. Some educational systems do cater for differences in learning capacity by requiring only part-time attendance from young children. In Scandinavia, for example, the seven-year-old attends for little more than half the time the school is open and only by the age of thirteen is he attending full-time.[2] By contrast, in English schools, five-year-old infants receive only one half hour per day less schooling than the adolescent school leaver. In this kind of situation, some teaching will inevitably wear the complexion of child minding or, from the pressure to fill a school day with educational activity, we impose conventional expectations of achievement upon the child irrespective of his individual potential. One of the problems raised by the anti-preparationist's insistence upon the importance of the child's deriving present satisfaction from education is the likelihood that in the case of many children this could be derived from no schooling at all, or going only occasionally, or for part of the day. If present need or interest is our basic criterion of educational provision, there is no reason to suppose that for all children – or for any – we need to provide five hours of schooling, five days a week.

A second consequence of the institutionalization of education which leads to an emphasis upon premature anticipation of the child's future needs is the existence of pressures from interested parties who finance, administer, or claim the right to exercise choice or influence in schooling. Thus, politicians, education officers, industrialists, parents demand that the young learn skills, techniques, information, attitudes and values for which the child does not only feel little need or interest but which, on a realistic calculation of his capacities, he has little chance of understanding. The popular view of education as a national investment implies preparation and the imposition of curricula based on calculations of interested parties about the nation's future needs. It follows from stressing the social function of education that it is difficult to isolate the school from outside pressures of an undesirable kind. And even if we take a dubious view of the morality of preparing the learner to serve the national interest, unrealistic anticipation of the child's future needs is sometimes prompted by concern for *his own* best interests. For the pervasiveness of preparation as an educational aim is partly a consequence of the relatively low statutory leaving age of most educational systems. Until the end of the Second World War this had stood at fourteen in most industrialized nations. Because of this, and from the best of motives, teachers have often attempted to communicate the minimum of knowledge and skill required by the adult citizen. It is all very well to follow Rousseau's injunction to 'waste time' when the student (like Emile) will still be in receipt of full-time education as a young adult. But in the past, relatively few have been in this fortunate condition. Hence the concern of teachers to save time by anticipating the adult needs of the children they teach. In fact, Rousseau's *Emile* underlines the folly of trying to make the best of both worlds. To abstract his prescriptions about the education of the young child and to apply these irrespective of the later conditions of the child's education, is to ignore the fact that it was only the extension of Emile's formal education into his adult life which gave sense to Rousseau's prescription to waste time when the child is still young.

Thus, the resolution of the present-future dilemma in education is partly a matter of institutional reform in extending the period of compulsory schooling and making higher education available to larger numbers. It is difficult to escape the conclusion that if we are to be rid of some of the less intelligent practices of the traditional school and are to promote education which has maximum meaning for the learner as and when it happens, the extension of the period of compulsory education further into adolescence is essential. As one educational report has put it: 'the school leaving age has to be extended, not in order that we may teach more, but in order that we may teach what we now teach at the correct stage and not at an age based upon circumstances external to the laws of child development'.[3] When we are driven by the shortness of the period of compulsory schooling to emphasize preparation, disregarding the present, this itself encourages the notion that schooling completes education and that one can satisfactorily exist for a lifetime on the cultural capital acquired as a child.

SOCIOLOGICAL IMPEDIMENTS TO CHILD–CENTRED EDUCATION

Structural reforms aimed at the extension of the period of formal education would make it less justifiable to think of education in exclusively preparatory terms. But as the outcry of many teachers against proposals to raise the school leaving age indicates, for many children this could aggravate the problem of motivation, especially in default of changed attitudes towards the learner and our conception of the disciplines we expect him to acquire. Indeed, teachers' fears for the consequences of compulsorily extended schooling focus another major factor which helps to widen the theory-practice gap; namely, our failure to acknowledge the sociological impediments to learning which characterize many urban environments. Children often bring to school negative, even hostile attitudes towards education which are a product of the environments in which they live. Observers of 'lower working class' culture have noted the arbitrary nature of child-rearing practices in this sub-culture. This has clear implications for those child–centred approaches to education which require greater initiative from the child as agent of his own learning. A characteristic of arbitrary child nurture is the frequent use of categoric statements (for example, 'because I tell you', 'because I'm your father') dependence on which 'reinforces the personal at the expense of the logical, the impersonal or task-related. It limits the possibilities of future learning and of varied behaviour: it affects reactions to authority in general'.[4] Thus, educational theory which encourages learning through problem-solving and critical evaluation of authorities must be dissonant with expectations engendered in the home. The child encouraged to act independently at school may be punished at home for failing to do as he is told: prompted in school always to seek for reasons, the child's behaviour will be construed as insolent by those at home: 'lower class parents . . . are more concerned with good behaviour than with psychological states; they want obedience, cleanliness and neatness compared with the relatively greater middle class emphasis on such psychic states as curiosity, happiness and consideration'.[5] In this climate of arbitrary social relationships, authority has either to be repudiated or obeyed: it functions as a moral imperative and not hypothetically as advice to be tested for its efficacy in promoting one's own objectives. And the child who accepts this sort of arbitrary authority will become disposed to see his mistakes not as things from which he can learn, but as shortcoming which indicate only a need for greater 'training, instruction and obedience' if he is ever to get things right.[6]

If this sort of imperative, arbitrary family relationship favours an authoritarian climate in educational situations, it also sends the child to school with quite different language patterns from those which are the habitual media of communication in schools. Bernstein poses the educational implications of this problem of language as follows: 'A major dilemma confounds the education of the lower working-class pupil. Unlike the middle class pupil, he lacks the understanding of basic concepts; neither is he oriented to building his experience upon those concepts. Insightful generalization is difficult. His order of cognitive evaluation would indicate that drill methods are required, so that the elements for later conceptualization are gained. Although this is unfashionable, I suggest that where culture induces a relatively low level of conceptualization, association rather than *gestalt* learning in children is more efficient. . . . Simply, the lower working class pupil does not possess basic *information*. The passivity of the pupil makes him peculiarly receptive to drill methods, but resistant to active participation and co-operation'.[7] Gordon also suggests the probable need for 'direct tutoring' in order to effect any sort of transfer from school experiences to those of the child's life outside school.[8]

However, Bernstein himself casts doubt upon the extent to which the school can ultimately succeed in its task of educating the lower-working class child aside from a radical transformation of the social context in which it operates.[9] He concluded that 'by fourteen years of age many lower-working-class children have become "unteachable" '.[10] If this were true, it would not be surprising in view of the promise which the future holds for most of them. The soul-destroying work which many of them seem destined to perform and the appalling housing in which they are condemned to live must appear to them to mock at any conception of education conceived in terms of cultural improvement. These children and their parents are often condemned for their indifference to education, but the reproach lies rather upon an industrial society which conceives this state of affairs as unalterable, or which gives appropriate social reform a low order of priority through the allocation of resources to alternative and often trivial uses.

The educational implications of this are that we ought to stop pretending that in the face of this sort of sociological impediment education is possible at all. The knowledge and skills necessary for survival in the industrial slum are unlikely to be those communicated by the school but, rather, those picked up from life itself. Thus, it is not surprising that the civilized culture of the school is rejected as irrelevant. This phenomenon of social impediments to education is by no means novel: it is as old as popular education itself and teachers in the central areas of large industrial cities have always been aware of considerable resistance to the culture they have had to offer. At the same time, they have often experienced guilt at their failure to make headway, especially since any and every manifestation of uncivilized behaviour on the part of their charges is apt to meet with the criticism from the public at large, 'What are their teachers doing about it?' What is new in the present situation is the candour with which educational theorists and semi-official bodies are prepared to concede that in some environments the teacher has to face near insurmountable obstacles to education. The major contribution of the Newsom Report was that for the first time it brought semi-official recognition of the fact that in some urban environments education is virtually impossible in the absence of changes outside the schools themselves. That is, we can no longer ascribe the depressingly low educational standards and resistance to schooling evidenced in many inner-city schools to a failure of imagination or concern on the part of teachers.

It is especially true that the use of child-centred techniques and the realization of child-centred values in education requires a favourable sociological climate. In this connection, the interesting point about these educational insights derived from observations of the language and child-rearing habits of different social classes is that they confirm some of the conclusions of key figures in the child-centred educational tradition. A. S. Neill has conceded that 'freedom works best with clever children. I should like to be able to say that, since freedom primarily touches the emotions, all kinds of children – intelligent and dull – react equally to freedom. I cannot say it'.[11] Nathan Isaacs drew a similar conclusion about the inapplicability to working class children of those educational methods which focus upon children's interests and assume the existence of that lively curiosity upon which child-initiated learning situations must depend: 'for those under the economic and other pressures of our poorer classes . . . there seems to be an air of mockery about "epistemic" or "causal" interest in their case. Cognitive development remains overlaid in them by all the environmental pressures and usually gets no chance at all of emerging, beyond the minimum adaptation required for survival, as an independent, voluntary interest'.[12] Isaacs drew this conclusion in his Appendix to the work in which Susan Isaacs described her

13

experimental school at the Malting House. She too acknowledged the importance of the favourable sociological context in which the school functioned: 'The children were from professional families, many of highly distinguished parents. They were all above the average mental ratio and ranged from 114 to 166, with a mean of 131.'[13] But as well as having this intellectually homogeneous middle class clientele, avid to learn in a way which facilitated the use of discovery, child-initiated learning situations, the material conditions at the Malting House were also much more favourable than in most publicly maintained schools. The staffing ratio, for example, was of a generosity unimaginable in the average school.

THE LIMITATIONS OF EXPERIMENTAL EDUCATION

Consequently, experimentalists often warn of the dangers of attempting to apply child–centred methods and values in the very different and limiting conditions which characterize most publicly provided schools.[14] Susan Isaacs herself believed that 'really to let the child learn by doing would involve an immense advance in all the material setting of school life, as well as in the number of staff and variety of equipment'. And elsewhere she concluded categorically that 'there is little to be done with large classes of children, ranging in ability from the nearly defective to the very superior, but to keep them quiet and talk to them . . . the children's need for real activity offers the chief justification for smaller classes'.[15] A major disincentive to the adoption of a thoroughgoing individualism in education is undoubtedly the size of classes. The notion of to each child his own curriculum would confront the teacher with problems of preparation, administration and supervision which appear insurmountable, given classes of the usual size. As we noted in Chapter 2, the most we contemplate in this direction is an attack upon the individual educational limitations of the backward child through streaming into fairly homogeneous ability groups and keeping remedial classes small.

It is because the unorthodox educational methods associated with child-centred education have often been devised in the favourable contexts provided by private experimental schools[16] that some educationalists have argued that child-centred practices cannot be widely applied within the public sector of education, a conclusion which seems only to be underlined by the occasional untypical and, hence, noteworthy occurrence of such practices within the maintained schools. Indeed, private education is sometimes defended, against the charge that it constitutes an immoral privilege, on the grounds that the private sector alone preserves conditions where educational innovation is possible: that is, if private education cannot be justified on grounds of social equity, perhaps intrinsically educational grounds can be adduced in justification of its preservation. This is an odd sort of defence of private education. For one thing, to argue that experiment can only flourish in private schools is not to demonstrate that the vast majority of private schools are anything but traditional and pedestrian in their methods. Moreover, the value of experimental private schools to the educational system at large is lost if we take at their word the notable experimentalists who concede that the results of experiments are only really applicable to the contexts in which they occur.

Nevertheless, it is true that prominent educational theorists have often concluded that their ideas can be implemented only in private institutions.[17] This preference for private over public institutions is partly a function of the economics of education. Only where people are prepared privately to finance a particular kind of education for their children can there be schools with values, organization and methods which depart radically from conventional expectations of what a school should be: 'Must not the school of the future . . . be able to support itself and so escape from the tyranny of money? He who pays commands! He who needs no alms is free!'[18] In publicly provided schools, taxpayers who pay the piper will expect to call the tune. They are usually on the side of economy in public expenditure and their collective expectations of what a school should be must approach the lowest common denominator of culture and taste. (Only recently a hostile television interviewer condemned the Deputy Chief Education Officer of Manchester for his authority's decision to set up an experimental primary school to implement proposals in the Plowden Report.) In our discussion of social education we noted that parents who wish their children to be educated in accordance with social and religious values upon which there is little consensus within the community must opt for private or voluntary schools. Maintained schools, whose populations embrace children from widely differing cultural backgrounds, must seek to achieve a normative consensus which probably makes for educational conservatism and 'safety first'. Moreover, whilst the child-centred tradition is anti-didactic, those looking for value for their money expect that children will be *taught* something. They are likely to be impatient with learning through play and with those educational 'frills' which, in the popular mind, child-centred schools seem to encourage at the expense of adequate standards of literacy and numeracy. And however mistaken this conception of child-centred theory may be, teachers in publicly provided schools are apt to be sensitive to the charge that anything they do is a threat to traditional educational standards, particularly in the 3Rs. There have been notable exceptions to this generalization about the conservative nature of the maintained school, but only such few exceptions as seem to prove the rule. Exceptional head teachers can convince parents, administrators, industrialists and other interested parties that 'experiment' with unconventional methods is proper and acceptable.

One further problem of applying theories which have been developed in experimental situations is focused by Susan Isaacs' disclaimer that the intention of her book was 'in large part psychological rather than educational'.[19] It is interesting that despite this expressed intention to speak to psychologists rather than to teachers, Mrs Isaacs could be constantly detected in the act of drawing educational generalizations from her observations: her declaration of her intention to offer mainly psychological theory tends to be lost in the midst of a discussion which frequently assumes an educational significance. This point is not of merely historical interest. There is a continuing tendency among psychologists (whether intentional or not) to smuggle educational prescriptions into their writings under the cover of disclaimers of anything but psychological intention. For example, it is often said of Piaget that he was not primarily interested in educational problems. Certainly, there are few direct references to schooling in his published work. Nevertheless, Piagetian inspired research is the educational growth industry and considerable effort goes into the task of making Piaget's findings available to teachers. As a departure from learning theory based upon observation of animals, the Piagetian tendency to focus upon children is to be welcomed. But this has to be a guarded welcome. For it is not merely, as with the experimental schools we have noted, that children in Piagetian situations are working either in small groups or in a one-to-one relationship with an adult observer: the problem with Piaget is rather that his inferences about stages of intellectual development are derived from observation of children in spontaneous, non-educational learning situations.

Thus, when prescribing educational innovation on the basis of psychological research it is important to remember that some of the more popular studies of children's learning have occurred in situations which are rarely reproduced in the classroom, particularly in maintained schools. Yet, for teachers, the crucial question about intellectual (or moral or emotional) development is how this might be encouraged in distinctively educational situations; that is, in the context of the school where there is a deliberate intention to cultivate the child's personal powers. If teachers are to be asked to modify their teaching in response to the findings of educational research, they clearly have a right to expect that experiments should be conducted in conditions which more nearly replicate the conditions in which they have to do their daily work.[20] The educational psychologist must forsake his 'laboratory' for the school; the experimental school must be assessed in the light of the favourable conditions under which it works. This point is of some current importance in view of the increasing tendency towards official sponsorship of educational research directed towards discovering how children learn. Either research must be undertaken as far as possible in conditions approximating to those in which children will necessarily be grouped in schools or, if experiment is with children in privileged groups, the community must will the resources which are needed to reproduce such conditions throughout the educational system. Any radical discrepancy between conditions under which research is carried out and the situation in which it is applied must vitiate its findings.

EDUCATIONAL THEORY AND THE ATTITUDES OF TEACHERS

However, it would be a mistake for teachers to conclude that because the values of child-centred education have been most fully realized in the private sector of education, child-centred educational theory has no pertinence to the work of the hard pressed practitioner in publicly maintained schools. He will rightly suspect some of the more extreme advocacy of child-centred education: those prescriptions, for example, which suggest that we can only do what is right by standing existing practice on its head, or those attempts to persuade us that nothing which follows from the new way of looking at things (for example, the Piagetian way) also follows from the old. This radical approach to educational change has a superficial logical attraction but it takes no account whatever of the psychology of teachers. When told that the implication of a particular educational theory is that they must abandon everything to which they are accustomed, teachers are unlikely to respond enthusiastically if only from the sense of insecurity which must follow from abandoning, completely and irrevocably, the familiar landmarks in curriculum, method and educational values. Few of us are temperamentally fitted for the business of burning bridges. We experiment and mend our ways tentatively, from securely held positions. And the certain way of getting no change at all is to suggest that change must be revolutionary. Some professional pride is also involved. It is difficult to give a sympathetic hearing to those who tell us that our existing practices are, and always were, utterly mistaken. Moreover, it is arguable that the piecemeal Fabian reform of the practitioner constitutes the only really scientific approach to the problem of change. On this view, intelligently conducted change is that which introduces novelty on such a modest scale that innovation can be evaluated step by step and experiments abandoned, or further modifications made, in the light of available evidence. But when all existing practices are swept away, it is not possible to reverse the process if innovation threatens to be unworkable. Of course, in the real world in which teachers live, this is the way in which innovation is engineered. Revolutionary Utopian prescriptions are rarely implemented. Their value as educational polemics lies, rather, in performing the valuable service of stopping us in our tracks and prompting the sort of heart-searching in which every committed and responsible practitioner becomes engaged from time to time.

However, as any teacher of educational theory knows, the danger of cautioning a circumspect approach to theory is that this is precisely the advice which confirms the lazy, conservative, unenterprising teacher in his conviction that the patient is as healthy as may be expected and that all education really needs is fewer 'do-gooders', critics, advisors and theorists to disturb the teacher's peace of mind. It has been our argument that the theory-practice gap derives, in part, from the Utopian and unsubtle character of much educational theorizing. But it is also a fact that the distance between the practical and the ideal varies considerably from school to school. It is a commonplace to those who supervise student teachers in a variety of schools that what is dismissed as impossibly theoretical in Shcool A is a daily occurrence in School B on the other side of town: in this respect there are even significant differences between classrooms in the same school. The limitations of School A often result from those sociological impediments to learning which the school itself cannot ameliorate. Even loss of teacher morale may derive from intolerable environmental pressures. But the failure of imagination which characterizes those who teach in School A often has no such obvious sociological justification, and the pretence that the gap which they observe between theory and practice follows from the unrealistic Utopianism of educational theorists is difficult to sustain. For one thing, few of those who teach educational theory in training institutions are educational innovators. Most novel methods originate in the schools and those who propagate them in training establishments are merely engaged in advocacy of what the best practitioners already do.

THE PRIMACY OF EDUCATIONAL PRACTICE

What the theorist has to learn to offer to the practitioner is a different conception of the role of theorizing in relation to the applied situation. Thus, in attempting to disentangle the strands built into the complex notion of child-centred education, we have not been engaged primarily in an attempt to discover which child-centred prescriptions might be rejected as mistaken, as against those which can safely and effectively be implemented. In discussing the meaning of child-centred education we have been attempting to fashion tools with which the practitioner might analyse his practice. So far as the rejection of educational theory by practitioners is a consequence of the way in which this has often been related to practice, it is important that we come to regard theory not as something we *apply*, in the sense of implementing a plan or blueprint, but as an instrument with which we explore and evaluate our practice. There is need for a re-orientation of educational theory so that we begin with the problems of the practical situation. We need to assert the primacy of the practical. Education is a practical activity and the *raison d'être* of educational theory in teacher training must be to equip the practitioner to understand the nature of the enterprise in which he is engaged.

The value of educational theory, then, lies primarily in enabling teachers to explore existing situations in order to understand exactly why they do what they do. It is sometimes necessary to recognize and admit that one does things in educational situations for what, from a purely educational point of view, are the wrong reasons: we should sometimes be prepared to concede that from outside pressures we do things in the classroom which are not in the best interests of the children we teach, rather than attempting to rationalize the indefensible. This may be the beginning of wisdom, since theories are then seen not as magic formulae for transforming classrooms overnight, but as signposts to the direction in which we ought to travel, given that we have the appetite or the will to change.

Even English teachers who suffer few formal administrative constraints on their freedom are rarely in a position to wipe the educational slate clean and begin teaching afresh according to their own conceptions of what is educationally desirable. Like the Irishman who was asked the way by a travelling stranger, most of us would, ideally, take a different point of departure. Teachers work in situations with many and varied historical antecedents which require compromise if anything is to be achieved at all. As we are coming increasingly to realize, some of our educational ills have such deep sociological roots that only in the company of related social reforms can we begin to pluck them out. But although many practical factors exist to hinder the pursuit of what seems theoretically desirable, these sociological factors are not immutable. And an essential function of educational theory remains to signpost the direction in which we ought to travel in pursuit of an education conceived in the best interests of the child.

REFERENCES

1 See KANT's essay 'On the saying "That may be all right in theory but is no good in practice" ' in G. RABEL *Kant*, Clarendon Press, Oxford, 1963: 'A set of rules, presented in a certain generality and with disregard of particular circumstances is called a *Theory* . . . The practitioner must exercise his *judgement* to decide whether a case falls under a general rule.'
2 See, for example, A. NELLEMANN *Schools and Education in Denmark*, p. 21. Det Danske Selskab, Copenhagen, 1964. Much the same is also true for Norway and Sweden.
3 Council for Curriculum Reform *The Content of Education*, p. 182. University of London Press, 1945.
4 J. KLEIN *Samples from English Cultures*, Vol. II, p. 519. Routledge & Kegan Paul, London, 1965. See also J. E. GORDON 'The Disadvantaged Pupil' *Irish Journal of Education*, Vol. II, No. 2.
5 GORDON, op. cit., p. 75.
6 KLEIN, op. cit., pp. 524–5.
7 B. BERNSTEIN 'Social Class and Linguistic Development:

a Theory of Social Learning' in A. H. HALSEY, J. FLOUD
and C. A. ANDERSON *Education, Economy and Society*,
p. 306. The Free Press, 1961.

8   GORDON, op. cit., p. 77.

9   BERNSTEIN, op. cit., p. 301, and GORDON, op. cit., p. 101.

10 BERNSTEIN, op. cit., p. 307.

11 NEILL *Summerhill*, pp. 112–13. Put in this way, it may
appear that one is equating lack of intelligence with
membership of the lower working class. What one does
have in mind here is the growing literature which
demonstrates some positive correlation between effective
or functional intelligence (e.g., as shown in capacity to
benefit from schooling) and the sociological environment
of the child.

12 N. ISAACS 'Children's "Why" Questions', pp. 347–8.

13 S. ISAACS *Intellectual Growth in Young Children*, p. 14.

14 See, for example, SCHOENCHEN *The Activity School*,
pp. vii, 289.

15 S. ISAACS *The Psychological Aspects of Child Development*,
p. 41. Evans Bros., London, 1963.

16 In this connection one recalls the work of Dewey's experimental school in Chicago.

17 W. BOYD *The History of Western Education*, pp. 318, 349.
A. & C. Black, London, 1952.

18 FERRIERE *The Activity School*, p. 260.

19 S. ISAACS *Intellectual Growth in Young Children*, p. 1.

20 It is interesting that one educational psychologist who
turns increasingly to the study of children and teachers
inside the classroom should display a refreshing candour
about the unrealistic nature of the prescriptions which
theorists have offered the teacher: see P. W. JACKSON
Life in Classrooms, Ch. 5.

12: Conclusion: Learner-centred education

It is a fundamental assumption of child-centred educationists that learning should have *meaning* for the child. Related terms like 'relevance', 'importance', 'significance' recur in the literature of this tradition and, especially, in the conversation of educationists. The point of educational activity is to enable the child to grasp the meaning of what he is attempting to learn. Unless the child understands what he learns, it remains a meaningless formula, a collection of inert ideas, a rote skill having no application outside the classroom situation in which it was learned. This is to say that education should be child-centred in that the learner comes to possess what he knows. His learning becomes a disposition to behave in a certain kind of way. In Polanyi's sense of the term, he has *personal knowledge*.[1] And having learning as a personal possession entails that the learner must know how to do something with his knowledge, though its practical value need not be merely instrumental in the sense of having social or economic utility (see pp. 122–6). The utilization of knowledge will often occur in subsequent learning situations within the school itself, and the competences acquired by the child will often be the skilled use of concepts, facts and principles as well as the mastery of motor skills. Knowing how to use concepts and apply principles in activities which are primarily theoretical is of no less importance than acquiring skill in practical affairs. But whether our concern is with learning how to perform motor, diagnostic or theoretical skills, the tacit element at the heart of all skills requires that the learner should practise them for himself. He cannot enter into possession of a skill merely by being *told* what to do. For this reason, we concluded that learning by doing is essential to the acquisition of knowledge as a personal possession[2] (see pp. 151-3).

The child must come to possess what he learns also in the sense that what he knows ought not to be particular to the situation in which it was learned but transferable to novel situations. Though an activity may be enjoyable in and for itself, its edcuational justification depends upon its relevance for experience outside the context in which it was learned. So far as his education assists in the solution of life's problems as he sees them as a child, it is because these are identifiable as examples of problems (moral dilemmas, for example) which have more than a local significance in time and place. Education for life should offer competences and disciplines whose power informs the whole of life (see Chapter 7, especially pp. 137-9).

A third necessary condition for bringing the child into possession of his learning is that his schooling should be related to his *own* experience, to his weaknesses as well as his strengths. The teacher must account for the learner's experience in the sense of discovering his personal growth points and using the concrete daily life occurrences within the child's environment as exemplar situations out of which abstract concepts and principles are forged (see Chapter 5, pp. 89-92). In Whitehead's terminology (see Appendix, pp. 213ff.), life as the child sees it is caught up in the romance stage of learning: it is also the arena in which the generalization of learning ultimately occurs. As we have argued in Chapter 2, relating education to the individual's own strengths and limitations does not require the provision of a unique curriculum for every child, but the educational point of departure for any child (or group of children) must take account of his personal history and the cultural privileges or deprivations which have made him what he is (see pp. 128-31 and Chapter 10). And although his balanced development as a person may require that he attends to the whole spectrum of human knowledge and experience, when the basic concepts and tools of learning are mastered, personal idiosyncrasies – individual talents, interests and dispositions – ought legitimately to determine the specialized directions which learning can take, either within or between distinctive curriculum activities.

Most of this could be agreed even by educationists who would never describe themselves as learner-centred. It would characterize efficient education in any school or college: an education where learners succeed in taking skill and knowledge into themselves so that what is learned may be employed successfully in the business of living and, to that end, where teachers take full account of personal and social impediments to learning and forge educational instruments to overcome these. There is this obvious sense in which all education is learner–centred in being conceived so that the learner will learn. Pupils may fail to learn, but the intention is always that they should acquire skills, attitudes, dispositions, knowledge. Even a so-called society-centred approach to education has this ultimate concern with the learner. Thus, education which springs from social assumptions like the need for economic efficiency, the importance of supplying industry with trained manpower, or the need to sustain the integrity of the State will ultimately require evaluation in terms of the skill and dedication with which the products of the educational system pursue these social values. So far as these ends are achieved, and so far as their realization depends upon the educational system, this will be because learners have acquired the appropriate social and economic skills and can exercise them efficiently. Whatever the educational aim, its achievement depends upon how efficiently learners acquire and practice the relevant skills. If this is so, the teacher's attention can never ultimately be focused anywhere than upon the learner. A teacher (for example, in a university) may believe his prime responsibility is to his discipline; that is, he may see himself first and foremost as a scholar. But so far as he *teaches*, success in this enterprise must be judged by reference to whether and how the learner learns. Thus, at least in this technical sense, all good teaching is learner-centred.

However, we have seen that the rationale of child-centred education goes beyond this problem of attending to the learner's peculiar strengths and limitations in order to promote efficient learning at a technical level. The moral impetus to the child-centred tradition derives from liberal–democratic ideology: the rights of man must be extended to the child (see Chapter 1). But again, many educationists who would not identify themselves as child-centred educationists would also stress the importance of moral considerations in according rights to children. It is not enough for most teachers that the procedures we adopt in schools should be technically efficient; they must also be consistent with our moral expectations of how other persons ought to be treated. As R. S. Peters puts it: 'To say that we are educating people commits us to morally legitimate procedures.'[2] From their regard for this moral dimension to education, most educationists are child-centred, for example, in deploring sadistic forms of punishment, or the belittling of children who cannot retort in kind, or the teacher who always takes it for granted that the unsuccessful learner must be stupid and who never entertains the possibility that failure in the classroom sometimes stems from his own professional inadequacy. Even educationists who (like Herbart) are sometimes categorized as teacher-centred because of their emphasis upon *instruction* are rarely indifferent to the claims of children to consideration as persons. To question 'happiness' as an educational aim is not to be committed to the view that children should be deliberately made unhappy in school (see Chapter 1). Or to be subject-centred in stressing the need for children to submit to the discipline of learning things which other people judge to be of value is not to deny that the end of the educational process should be personal autonomy. Educationists who believe, like R. S. Peters, that the initiation of children into worthwhile interests may go against the grain of the learner's present inclinations contend that, ultimately, to be on the inside of these activities is to be a rational autonomous being.[3] The essential difference between this and the more extreme advocacy of child-centred education is the latter's stress upon the possibility of the child's autonomy as a person *whilst he is still a learner*. It is not merely that in the interests of technically efficient learning the learner has a right to participate in a conversation with his teacher, to require reasons and express his own judgements and evaluations. The assumption is that as well as being competent to feed back to his teacher the information necessary to clarify his difficulties and focus his educational needs, he also has the right to design and engineer his own education (see Chapter 8). Life as *he* sees it, his own conception of what he needs and his own present interests should be the point of departure of his education.

This is the point at which many educationists part company with the child-centred tradition. A learner-centred education which starts from the child's own spontaneous experiences and interests and is limited by his present capacity for understanding carries dangers of subjectivity and may merely confirm the child in his immaturity, his prejudices and his cultural poverty (see Chapters 5 and 7). On this view, it is important that the links which are made with the lives of the culturally deprived in our schools are merely instrumental: that is, are means to facilitate the mediation of some vision of the good life which may be alien to the culture in which they live. Motivation intrinsic to the experience of the learner may dispose him towards activity having no educational value. This, no less than the learner's potential for culturally valuable development, is a part of the educational frame of reference. Critics of child-centred education are rarely calling for a return to the meaning-less rote procedures which often characterized learning in the traditional school. Their reservations about the wisdom of this concentration upon the child's present capacities and interests are intended to emphasize that education should enlarge the range, the areas, or the 'realms' of meaning available to the child. From this point of view, the learner's attention should be directed towards meanings which are significant for living in a civilized culture. The child's education should point him towards the *best* available culture (see pp. 131–9). Thus, in the child's own interests, we need the concept of the teacher as an authority (see pp. 61–73).

As authority, it is the teacher's responsibility to indicate the possible limitations of the learner's own spontaneous and un-tutored choice of activity, to mediate the vision of a wider, richer environment. He prompts the learner to ask himself if what he wants to learn is really worth learning in relation to the avail-able alternatives: is his choice really in his best interests? Left to pursue his own inclinations the child may choose subject matter which is of little cultural value, which may even reinforce his cultural deprivation. Thus, even in a liberal climate where the child is permitted considerable free choice of activity, the teacher has an obligation to make quite explicit what the child's own choice implies in cultural terms. What are the limitations which it imposes upon future learning? How many cultural or professional doors are closed by a particular curriculum choice and how much sweat and tears are implied in one which keeps them open? As authority, the teacher's competence also lies in his obligation to assess the disciplinary implications of a child's choice of educational activity: does it pose an unrealistic challenge in failing to stretch the child or in requiring from him disciplined activity of which he is probably incapable? And once the child is embarked upon an activity, the teacher's disciplinary role is to encourage persistence when the romance of learning is overshadowed by the need for precision. At this stage, the teacher insists upon proper attention to detail, to the 'grammar' of learning. As was argued above (see pp. 66–73), self-discipline is the product of an education: to ignore the teacher's legitimate disciplinary function is to assume that the child has the capacity to discipline himself from the start, thus making schooling redundant.

This cautionary, disciplinary, advisory, evaluative function will, indeed, involve the teacher in a thorough knowledge of the individual learner's capacities, interests and aspirations. But the place where he finds the child is also relative to where he might wish to go and this, in turn, has implications for the skills and concepts he needs to acquire in order to travel purposefully and with a sense of direction. To this end it is important that the teacher is familiar with the map of knowledge as well as with the intentions, the talents and the stamina of the traveller. Thus it is important to resist pressures to over-balance the teacher's training towards his 'professional' at the expense of his 'academic' education (see Chapter 10). Mention of this third item in the educational nexus – the disciplined organization of our knowledge of the universe – is also a reminder of the danger of attaching undue importance to personal relationships in education and underplaying the purpose for which persons come together in educational institutions. If authority is not to degenerate into authoritarianism, part of the child's safeguard lies in the existence of the academic disciplines. It is important that the teacher, no less than the learner, is under the discipline of something outside himself. The learner thus has a court of appeal beyond his teacher, not to another personal opinion, but to a public body of fact, principles and technical procedures. The possibility of reference to public criteria and standards of this sort is prophylactic against both the learner's disposition towards egocentrism and the authoritarian potential of the teacher's role. Moreover, we have argued that disciplines provide the learner with the instruments of self-discipline at the point when he is competent to dispense with the authority of his teacher. Indeed, his grasp of the discipline is the index of his readiness to launch out alone.

But from the point of view of the learner, locating learning situations within the academic disciplines has disadvantages. Through the slogan, 'We teach children, not subjects' (see pp. 96–9), child-centred educationists have often been drawing attention to the dangers of valuing academic disciplines for their own sakes (see pp. 126–8). Teachers need to be sensitive to the obsolescence of knowledge and to seize opportunities for the creation of new areas of study, whether by synthesis or division, as the development of science or the practical interests of men require it. One aspect of the protest against the traditional subject curriculum has related to the insistence upon preserving classical modes of explaining phenomena when these are no longer appropriate, and the refusal to accommodate new interests. Again, the failure to recognize the disciplinary values of many activities which lie outside the conventional preoccupations of the European middle classes needs correction (see pp. 133–6). Disciplines must also be conceived developmentally in relation to the child's developing capacities. They require analysis in terms of key concepts and principles which are capable of illustration from the learner's own experience. The teaching of educational disciplines does not involve dilution of remote adult experiences, so much as application of fundamental principles to data of increasing complexity as the learner's experience grows (see pp. 89–92). This developmental concept of the disciplines is particularly relevant to the objection that subject studies are inappropriate in the education of the less able child. One recalls Bruner's claim that 'good teaching that emphasizes the structure of a subject is probably even more valuable for the less able student than for the gifted one'.[4]

As well as adopting a developmental view of subject teaching, other safeguards are necessary to forestall the charge that the academic disciplines embody 'inert ideas'. Their relationship with other disciplines and their relevance for life experience needs to be made explicit. The integrated type of cross-disciplinary study is one method of achieving this; but subject teaching itself provides opportunity for exemplifying the interrelatedness of disciplines one with another and with human experience outside the academic context (see pp. 112–16). The manner in which the disciplines are taught is an important determinant of how far they contribute towards self-discipline, mitigate authoritarianism and assist transfer of learning. Exploration of material for its power to illumine life outside the classroom invites the learner to participation in a discussion. Though life as he sees it can never determine curriculum content, the teacher who is interested in the child's observations on life is committed to a conversation (see p. 165) which diminishes his tendency to resort to authoritarian devices of declamation, dictation, narration, description in the spirit of 'brooking no argument', and without reference to the effect which these activities are having upon children.

With these provisos, the term 'academic discipline' assumes its proper function of picking out those culturally valuable activities (practical as well as theoretical) whose nurture requires the professional expertise of teachers, as distinguished from those activities which are best learned from other educational agencies like the home, or are learned from life in the daily commerce of the market place (see pp. 85–6). Although the word is used habitually in a derisory sense, 'academic' ought to refer descriptively to that special kind of learning which prompts the community to devote some of its scarce resources to the provision of 'academies' or schools.

This conclusion that the educational nexus is triadic – that

children require authoritative teachers and a curriculum carefully devised for its cultural and disciplinary values – should be
an obvious one, but it is apt to be ignored in a great deal of
educational discussion which, as we observed in the introduction,
confronts us with nothing but exclusive alternatives. We too
readily accept that educationally we are always on the horns of a
dilemma, preferring the disjunctive 'or' to the conjunctive 'and'.
The simple notion that the child, the teacher and the curriculum
are educational co-efficients eludes us in our single-minded
disposition towards monism.

There are educationists who take it for granted that educational theory must assume the aspect of a conflict rather than a
disinterested search for truth. Riesman, for example, has suggested that 'it would be helpful to develop a systematic theory
of education as *counter-cyclical*', on the model of Keynesian
economics.[5] From this viewpoint, in a period dominated by
concern for the child, theorists would assert the claims of the
disciplines and the authority of teachers. Upon Dickensian-type
schools, the values of spontaneity, initiative, freedom and
problem solving would be urged against sterile preoccupation
with facts. Out of this, it is hoped, would emerge a satisfactory
synthesis, a stabilizing of educational practice at a point mid-
way between the extremes to which the pendulum swings.
Unfortunately for the protagonists of this argument, the teacher
(the hub about whom the pendulum moves) contemplates both
extremities with distaste, leaves the theorists at their play and
carries on with the daily task of teaching children. For, as the
most recent British example of counter-cyclical educational
thinking shows[6], this sort of theorizing is conducted with scant
regard for the facts and in a way which only drives us all back
to our entrenched positions. Dewey (who once favoured the
counter-cyclical approach) came to realize that eventually the
theorist becomes the prisoner of his own polemic, tending to
develop his 'principles negatively rather than positively and
constructively'.[7] There can be no gain, least of all for children,
when educational theory is conceived as a perpetual conflict.
For the middle ground is not a neutral territory where reasonable men come together to fashion a treaty of peace; it is a

no-man's-land where virtually nothing of rational educational theory survives at all.

REFERENCES

1   POLANYI *Personal Knowledge,* and see pp. 128–31 above.
2   R. S. PETERS *The Concept of Education,* p. 3.
3   R. S. PETERS *Education as Initiation.*
4   BRUNER *The Process of Education,* p. 5.
5   D. RIESMAN 'Thoughts on Teachers and Schools' *The Anchor Review,* No. 1.
6   The *Black Paper.*
7   J. DEWEY, *Experience and Education,* pp. 1–7.

Appendix:
A note on *Whitehead's* principle of rhythm in education

Whitehead claims no originality for his belief that education is a cyclical process in which different but recurring emphases are necessary if learning is to fructify. But what is peculiarly suggestive is the terminology he uses to categorize the phases of the cycle: *romance, precision* and *generalization*. These are elaborated in Chapters II and III of *The Aims of Education*, but since reference to the terms has been made in a number of different contexts (see pages 111, 114–15, 147, 164–5 and 204 above), a brief outline of their implications may be helpful.

Romance is a stage in which the context of what is to be learned is explored. What is its relevance, importance, interest, usefulness to the learner? How does it fit into wider aspects of the subject and of human knowledge? How does it link with the existing experience, knowledge, concerns, aspirations, fears and value systems of the learner? Does what is to be learned have exciting implications? Above all, why should the learner trouble himself to learn this particular information or skill? The stage of romance, therefore, constitutes an attempt to gain perspective by standing back from the minutiae of a subject or skill. In Whitehead's own phrase, it means grasping things 'in the rough' before smoothing out and shaping them through attention to detail. In order to acquire learning we must first shake ourselves free of it. And this stage is more than mere titillation. It is a genuine whetting of appetite rather than a sugaring of pills. Again, in Whitehead's own terms, romance means the setting in ferment of the mind, the creation of a mood of adventure. It is from romance that the learning experience gains its 'affective tone'. Knowledge is never 'mere knowledge'. It 'is always accompanied with accessories of emotion and purpose'[1] and it is from the stage of romance that the learner gains his 'concern' for what he is to learn.

At the stage of precision the learner comes to grips with detail. He learns information. He is involved in 'analysing the facts bit by bit', submitting where necessary, to the discipline of drill and repetition: 'In this stage, width of relationship is subordinated to exactness of formulation. It is the stage of grammar, the grammar of language and the grammar of science'.[2] All this is as necessary to the learning situation as the superficially more enjoyable stage of romance. Learning dominated by romance 'lacks the restraint which is necessary for the great stage of precision.'[3] At this stage comes the recognition that in almost any business of life – professional, political, domestic, leisured – 'things have been found out and . . . to be effective in the modern world you must have a definite acquirement of the best practice. To write poetry you must study metre; to build bridges you must be learned in the strength of material. . . . The untutored art of genius is, in the words of the Prayer Book, a vain thing, fondly invented'.[4] Emphasis upon a stage of precision as necessary to any learning situation should disarm critics of child-centred education who complain of 'soft pedagogy'. For from this point of view, doctrines of interest and activity are not inconsistent with hard work, drill, repetition, attention to detail and even a degree of drudgery: 'I am not contemplating one beautiful lecture stimulating, once and for all, an admiring class. That is not the way in which education proceeds. No; all the time the pupils are hard at work solving examples, drawing graphs and making experiments, until they have a thorough hold on the whole subject.'[5]

But one important implication of the rhythm principle is that the precision of learning is only acceptable when set within a context of romance and generalization. Tedious mechanical work, repetition, drill, memorizing may be inescapable in learning, but these become acceptable only within a context of concern to learn for reasons beyond the drudgery itself: 'A stage of precision is barren without a previous stage of romance' and 'undiscriminating discipline defeats its own object by dulling the mind'.[6] Precision has to be a matter of making the pupil see the wood by means of the trees. But precision which is mere drill, drudgery for its own sake, has no place in education. Moreover, this stage is constantly open to the danger of being concerned with technique without principle. Yet the precision itself should contribute to the gaining of insight for which the larger learning cycle exists. Where romance has stimulated genuine interest and not merely provided a sugaring of the pill, precision is not an irksome stage, indispensable as a means to an end but contributing nothing intrinsically valuable to the experience. The transfer of learning – generalization – requires that technique shall have been acquired, as far as possible, by a process of understanding. That is, the precision of learning should be conducted with an eye to transfer value; with a stage of generalization in mind. Teachers may have to ask children to take certain things on trust pending a later deepening of understanding. Children may even enjoy drill and repetition as play; as activities without extrinsic reference. But if we expect transfer of the techniques we teach to situations outside those in which they are learned, precision must be related to generalization, the third stage of Whitehead's cycle.

Generalization need not be in some 'real life' situation outside the school. Attempts to bring the learning cycle to a stage of generalization will only issue in frustration if the concept of utilization of knowledge which it implies is construed too narrowly as a putting of what is learned to immediate use in the life of the market place outside the school. It is clear that while Whitehead saw this kind of application as important, the skills, concepts and techniques mastered at the stage of precision will often fructify in initiating another learning cycle, within the same subject or in relation to other aspects of the curriculum. Generalization will usually begin another cycle, thus constituting the stage of romance of the next cycle.

The stage of generalization, then, marks the fructification of learning: at this point the learner is aware of an access of power. What is learned is seen to be a means to ends beyond itself. The learner has not merely acquired new tricks: he sees what exactly

can be done with his new skill, concept, information. In Whitehead's view 'education is the acquisition of the art of the
utilization of knowledge'.[7] This application of learning may be
in the wider commerce of life or as an aid to further scholarship
within the school itself. What it ought not to be is mere erudi-
tion – an indulging in educational minuets, as Whitehead puts it.
As in the stage of romance detail is lost in the whole: 'details are
swallowed up in principles';[8] they are shed 'in favour of the
active application of principles'. Much of the material from the
stage of precision is latent knowledge of which we are only
subsidiarily aware. The importance of carrying through learning
to a stage of generalization is that it is prophylactic against the
danger of 'inert ideas': 'that is to say, ideas that are merely
received into the mind without being utilized, or tested, or
thrown into fresh combinations'.

Whitehead's own discussion of the implications of the
rhythmic cycle is mainly in terms of an educational lifetime. He
writes of the romance of infancy giving way to the precision of
childhood and issuing in generalization during adolescence
which, itself a stage of romance, initiates a fresh cycle. But
though Whitehead hinted at the possible application of the
cycle to any unit of learning – a single lesson as well as a
lifetime of education – few educationists have attempted to
exemplify the rhythmic stages concretely in relation to distinctive disciplines. However, one example of such a concrete
application of the principle to learning the skills of reading and
writing is that outlined by Roberts.[9]

The principle of rhythm in education is a valuable conceptual
tool for exploring values and resolving some of the dilemmas
which confront educationists at the level of both theory and
practice. In particular, it helps us to escape some of those false
dichotomies which, as we noted in our introduction, are the stuff
of which a great deal of educational theory is made. By positing
a learning activity in which three correlative functions are
present, Whitehead moves us away from a propensity to
manufacture educational dualisms and our almost inevitable
tendency to regard these as the horns of a dilemma.

REFERENCES

1 A. N. WHITEHEAD *Adventures of Ideas*, p. 12. Cambridge University Press, 1961.
2 A. N. WHITEHEAD *The Aims of Education*, p. 29.
3 Ibid., p. 35.
4 Ibid., p. 53.
5 Ibid., p. 15.
6 Ibid., p. 50.
7 Ibid., p. 6.
8 Ibid., p. 58.
9 G. R. ROBERTS *Reading in Primary Schools*, pp. 47–52. See also 'Writing Continuous Prose: Value of the Cyclic Process' *The Times Educational Supplement*, 30 April 1965.

Index